Libby Wilson is now retired from her career as a General Practitioner and reproductive health expert. As well as being the author of many medical reports and papers, her previous book **Unexpected Always Happen** (Argyll, 1995) is an account of a year spent working in Sierra Leone.

SEX
on the Rates

memoirs of a family planning doctor

Libby Wilson

Argyll
publishing

© Libby Wilson 2004

First published in 2004 by
Argyll Publishing
Glendaruel
Argyll PA22 3AE
Scotland
www.skoobe.biz

The author has asserted her moral rights.

British Library Cataloguing-in-Publication Data.
A catalogue record for this book is available from
the British Library.

ISBN 1 902831 70 5

Cover photo: John Birdsall www.JohnBirdsall.co.uk

Origination: Cordfall Ltd, Glasgow

Printing: Mackays of Chatham Ltd

To all those whose foresight, compassion and persistence established the family planning services that women are free to use today. They worked hard for little or no pay, no status and frequently faced opprobrium from society. Recognition by their patients more than compensated for the lack of it by their peers.

Only a few are mentioned by name in this book but hundreds of doctors, nurses and lay people founded, through the Family Planning Association, the professional and ethical standards that form the bedrock of present-day practice in reproductive health care. I am proud to be among them.

Contents

Glossary

Acronyms

FPA	Family Planning Association
IRA	Irish Republican Army
KCH	Kings College Hospital
NAAFI	Navy, Army, Air Force Institute
NHS	National Health Service
PDSA	People's Dispensary for Sick Animals
RCOG	Royal College of Obstetricians and Gynaecologists
SSAFA	Soldiers', Sailors' and Airmen's Families Association
WAAF	Women's Auxiliary Air Force

Contraceptive terms

Condom 'Durex', 'johnny bag', 'rubber'.

DP Depo-Provera. A contraceptive injection containing a progestogen.

Dutch Cap, 'Cap', Diaphragm Rubber or plastic cap-shaped diaphragm placed in the vagina to cover the cervix.

IUD Intra-uterine contraceptive device. Known as 'the coil' or 'the loop' or 'the shield'.

'Natural' Family Planning Using observations of bodily functions (temperature, mucous production etc) to estimate the time of ovulation and refrain from intercourse during that time.

Oral Contraception The use of synthetic hormones taken by mouth to prevent contraception.

The Pill An oral contraceptive, containing two hormones, an oestrogen and a progestogen. May also refer to the POP.

POP The Progestogen Only Pill which contains only one hormone, a progestogen.

Spermicide Chemical agent which kills sperm. Used with caps and on lubricated condoms.

Sterilisation Cutting or tying the fallopian tubes to prevent the transport of the egg to the uterus. Can also refer to Vasectomy (*vide infra*).

Vasectomy Male sterilisation by division or interruption of the *vas deferens*, the tube that carries the sperm from the testicle.

General medical terms

AID Artificial Insemination by Donor. The use of donated semen to effect conception, normally carried out in a medical facility.

AIDS Acquired Immune Deficiency Syndrome. A disease, usually sexually transmitted, in which there is severe loss of immunity to infections and some cancers – until recently always eventually fatal.

Cerebral tumour Cancer in the brain.

Cervical Cytology The microscopic study of cells from the cervix to detect cancerous or pre-cancerous changes.

Cervix The neck of the uterus which projects in the vault of the vagina.

Colposcopy Detailed examination of the cervix and removal of minute tissue samples for microscopic study.

Craniotomy Making a hole in the skull to examine the brain.

D&C Dilation and curettage. Stretching the cervical canal into the uterus to allow the curette (like a sharp-edged spoon) to scrape the inside and remove an early pregnancy or tissue for diagnosis.

Disseminated (Or Multiple) Sclerosis A chronic disease of the nervous system.

Haematology The study of the blood

Herpes 'Cold sore'. Blisters round the mouth or mucous membranes caused by the herpes virus.

HIV The Human Immunodeficiency Virus. The cause of AIDS

Hymen The membrane of thin skin, usually perforated by a fingertip-sized hole which protects the opening into the vagina and which ruptures on full intercourse.

Hysterotomy The removal of a foetus (usually of more than 13 weeks gestation) by surgically opening the uterus.

Malignant Hyperthermia A very high rise in body temperature, fatal if not reduced.

MB, BS   Bachelor of Medicine, Batchelor of Surgery
MD   Doctor of Medicine
MRCP   Member of the Royal College of Physicians
Paraldehyde A liquid narcotic and sedative.
Path Lab Pathology laboratory where detailed examination of body fluids and tissues are made.
Rodent ulcer Slow-growing cancerous ulcer of the skin which invades locally but does not spread to the rest of the body.
Seminal Analysis The microscopic examination of semen to assess the number and viability of the sperm.
Septicemia Blood poisoning.
Speculum The smooth, blunt instrument used to hold the walls of the vagina apart in order to examine the cervix or access the uterus.
Sphygmomanometer Used to measure the blood pressure by means of a cuff wrapped round the upper arm and inflated.
Thyrotoxicosis Illness resulting from overactivity of the thyroid gland.
Venereology The study of sexually transmitted diseases. Also known as genito-urinary medicine.

Other
Bunter of Greystoke A notoriously fat boy in school stories of the era.
Nyassaland Now Malawi.
Operation Overlord The invasion of Europe by the Allies during World War II
Panel patients Working men who paid National Insurance contributions. General practitioners were reimbursed for their medical care. Their wives and children were not included.
Nappy pins large safety pins used to hold together bulky terry towelling napkins.
PC   Politically correct
School Cert. The equivalent of the General Certificate of Education.
Wartime Currency Ten shillings = 50p; half a crown = 2/6 = 12.5p; florin = 2/- = 10p; Sixpence = 2.5p

Foreword

I cannot remember a time when I did not want to be a doctor. I was fascinated by the combination of the detective element required for diagnosis and the everyday involvement with humanity. Sherlock Holmes and my father combined to make medicine an inevitable choice of career. I had no ambitious plans to become a great surgeon or a consultant at a teaching hospital. I wanted to practise and took whatever opportunity was offered compatible with marriage to a high-flying medical academic and the birth and upbringing of six children.

Fate decreed that I should end up in Glasgow as Clinical Coordinator of Family Planning and Women's Health Services (which was a one-off title invented by Greater Glasgow Health Board to cover my lack of consultant status). I was medically responsible for virtually all the family planning and well-woman clinics in the City of Glasgow and for a home visiting service covering 3000 families. I managed to maintain my involvement in routine contact (the phrase 'hands-on' may be too literally true to be acceptable in these politically correct days) with patients in all aspects of this developing speciality. I enjoyed a full and varied professional life and in the course of this book hope to show that there is more to 'family planning' than writing prescriptions for 'the pill'.

I retired from work in the NHS in 1990, twelve months before my 65th birthday, to go and work in Sierra Leone. On my return a year later my ties with family planning and reproductive health had been cut, as I intended. I became involved with euthanasia and choices at the end of life, the logical progression from my earlier battles concerned with choice at its beginning. I have already written about my time in Africa and the final chapter is, I hope, not quite ready to be recorded.

There are important experiences which are, even now, too painful to expose; the death of a baby in 1955, the death of my husband before he was sixty, at the height of his eminence and influence and the realisation that being a widow renders one a non-person as far as one's social life is concerned.

I have learnt to 'put not my trust in princes'(or administrators). There have been four occasions when false words were spoken and promises were made which, even at the time, those in authority had no intention of honouring

During my time as Clinical Coordinator of Family Planning and Reproductive Health Services in Glasgow, a first rate cervical cytology service was established, followed by regular colposcopy clinics and two self referring menopause sessions. Every week forty men were counselled and subsequently operated upon by the vasectomy service, all within the NHS. Psychosexual counsellors became involved in treating transsexuals and those with gender problems. We had a flourishing 'natural' family planning session which was largely used, often successfully, by those wanting to conceive rather than those trying to prevent it. We had a very effective arrangement with the laboratory at the Western Infirmary for fresh seminal analyses and in the few cases where the man was virtually infertile, the couple might choose to be referred to the British Pregnancy Advisory Service who ran an effective Artificial

Insemination by Donor programme. Some of the children thus conceived are now at university.

We were involved in research projects, both scientific and sociological. Many, especially those involving clinical assessment of new oral contraceptives, were initiated by pharmaceutical companies. We were only part of a network of clinics enrolling patients and recording data. Nevertheless such trials were time consuming and demanding but were undertaken because we believed it was important that we should contribute to the reputable bank of knowledge that was being assembled about these new products. Several have stood the test of time and are still widely prescribed.

Dr Ronald Weir undertook an important independent study over a three year period in which he demonstrated conclusively that rises in blood pressure were significantly associated with the amount of oestrogen in the combined oral contraceptive pill and that progestogen only pills had no such effect. He was awarded his MD for this thesis. I have always thought these fundamental findings were not widely enough acknowledged. We were also instrumental in providing a base for research on precancerous changes in the cervix by Mr Henry Kitchener (now Professor of Gynaecological Oncology, University of Manchester) and many other research projects the results of which were published in various reputable medical journals.

I became involved in training days with the Strathclyde Police who were setting up a special unit of female officers to deal with rape and child abuse. It was essential for the women police officers to understand the main principles governing conception and the pathology of venereal diseases if they were to be able to help the victims of rape and abuse. I had been appalled by the manner in which rape victims were treated by the police and had expressed my disquiet to both the Chief Police Surgeon and the Deputy Chief Constable. Fortunately Inspector (subsequently Chief Inspector) Hood was newly returned from holding a Churchill scholarship in the USA to study better ways of dealing with sexual crimes. The new unit was the result and I was pleased to be included in their training.

I regularly visited girl's remand homes, while they still existed; children's homes; adult training centres and sheltered work shops. This gave me a special insight into the everyday problems of the disadvantaged in society which, I hope, I was able to convey in the teaching and training programmes with which I was involved for thirty years. Passing on one's knowledge and experience to the next generation is very rewarding but perhaps it is the attitude and manner in which we approaches our fellow men and women – colleagues, clients or patients – that is the more lasting legacy.

Looking back after more than twelve years absence, it is the people that I remember. The occasional heart-warming contact with some one who asks 'You are Dr Wilson, aren't you ?' followed by a happy recollection of advice given, ('keep away from the surgeons'), a story listened to ('you believed me when I told you. . .') a timely intervention ('you stopped me throwing her out of the house'). These are the facts that matter.

Doctors are extraordinarily privileged to be involved in people's lives but it is only rarely that we are subsequently made aware of the effect our transient contacts have had, unless we work in an old-fashioned general practice. All the reforms we initiated, the projects we started, the services we established become irrelevant as time passes but the human memories remain, at least as long as our brains are functioning and I haven't got Altzheimers yet!

Libby Wilson

February 2004

Early Days

I peered through the banisters of the upstairs landing and watched the blood drip from the young man's hand onto the pile of the red turkey 'runner' in the hall. He had come off his motorbike trying to turn the icy corner from South Norwood Hill into Whitehorse Lane. I watched as my mother (a trained nurse) wrapped the injured part in a white cloth and sat him down on a chair in the hall outside the consulting room, ('surgeries' were decades away). What happened next I do not know. I was only five at the time but even then I was fascinated by my father's profession and undeterred by the sight of blood.

I had overheard my Aunt Elsie, who was always an expert on any topic she happened to mention, congratulating my mother.

'How wise of you and Jim to buy this house on the corner. It's such a good position. The plate shows up very well.'

She and Uncle Charlie were comfortably established in relatively well-off Streatham where private patients were the norm and my uncle had no need to have panel patients on his books. My father, younger and not long back from Africa, was struggling to establish himself in general practice in a less affluent part of South London. They all knew the importance of **being noticed** without actually advertising. The brass plate was the nearest any doctor could get to a poster proclaiming his skills.

Unlike the hero of Conan Doyle's *Stark Munro Letters* my aunt did not spell out the advantages of living on a sharp corner halfway up a steep hill, but this hazard, literally on the doorstep, was a potential source of professional business as the young man's accident had demonstrated.

My father's restless spirit kept us on the move; we changed house every two years and by the time I was ten we were living in a pleasant part of South Croydon. I walked to school along Croham Road; the pavement separated from the school playing fields and the wooded hill of Croham Hurst by hedges of hawthorn and wild rose.

Why he suddenly 'felt the call of his native heath', as he described his decision to go and live in Aviemore, I never found out. He was Edinburgh born, bred and educated and the Highlands of Scotland had never been his native heath or that of his forebears. Nevertheless, off we all went in the spring of 1936 to Aviemore, then a small village thirty two miles from the nearest town, Inverness; twelve miles to the next village with a shop, with no electricity, let alone gas; cut off by road for days at a time by snow in winter and a basic population of only 700 for most of the year.

For my parents it was a near disaster from almost every point of view. General practitioners bought and sold the 'goodwill' of their practices and this represented a large portion of their capital. On his return from Nyassaland in 1926 my father had paid £10 to a drunken old doctor for his practice in Penge in South London. He had built this up and extended it into Norwood so that when we moved to South Croydon, the practice was worth a reasonable sum. The amount he paid for the 'goodwill' of the Aviemore practice had been excessive as, for most of the year, the income came from the far from generous salary provided by the Highlands and Islands

Medical Service. There were probably no more than a score of private patients in the entire district – the laird, the minister, the schoolmaster, the managers of the hotels and a handful of others. The five hotels filled up in the summer months but there was no winter skiing season then and most of the doctor's income had to be made from the summer visitors. He felt he could not mislead his possible successor as to the value of the 'goodwill' and his anxieties increased the longer he stayed.

These financial uncertainties worried him greatly and after two years we moved again but not before my brother, sister and I and numerous cousins and friends, had spent two magical summers, totally unaware of our parents' concerns. We explored the wild hills and moors round Rothiemurchus on our bikes, swam in the lochs, built dens in the forest, performed plays in the barn of a friendly farmer and climbed all the Cairngorms except Cairn Toul. We soaked up the local folklore, of which there was plenty, believing in the curse of the five stones on the grave of Angus Og in old Rothiemurchus churchyard and listening for the clang of the fairy bell at Inch, flying through the night on some healing mission. We tried to find the causeway across to the Wolf of Badenoch's castle on the island in Loch an Eilean but had to make do with the echo from the bank; we started to excavate an old burial mound near the road to Avielochan but desisted when the farmer told us it would be unwise to disturb the little folk. But by the summer of 1938 my father had had enough.

Throughout these changes in lifestyle, moving house six times in twelve years my mother managed the household, bore and brought up three children, coped with the 'servant problem' – much easier in Aviemore because Barbara lived out and came every day on her bicycle from Coylumbridge – and always had a welcome for all the friends and relations that spent a lot of their Easter and summer holidays with us. It was she who led the party, including six children of whom I and my school friend, Lorna, were the oldest at eleven, up Cairngorm (4000ft) following the 'tack' marks of the climbers' nailed boots, tying our jerseys round her waist as we ran ahead in our plimsolls in vests and kilts; she who mustered the bikes for picnics, dealt with ten brace of Arctic hare (what a pong in the scullery) and supported Jim through all the near sleepless nights, infrequent medical crises and the boredom of the long northern winter that were an inevitable part of a general practitioner's life in such an isolated place.

On one occasion my father took me to a tiny cottage of wood with a tar-paper roof – a 'butt 'n ben' – on the edge of the village. He knocked on the door that opened straight into a small dark little room where the old couple sat on either side of a smouldering peat fire that failed to counteract the overwhelming stench. I gulped as the smell hit me but my father seemed unaware. The old woman gave us tea and a soda scone, difficult to eat in the circumstances. When the courtesies were over the dressings were removed and the lesion exposed.

My father wanted me to see the huge rodent ulcer which had eaten away most of an ear and was ulcerating the side of the old man's face. Even in 1937 such malignancies could be successfully treated with radium and, as they do not spread to other parts of the body, the patient could have been cured. But old Mackenzie would not go to hospital, not even to Inverness, which he had visited only once or twice. There was no persuading him and I hope he died of pneumonia, the 'old man's friend' before the ravages of the cancer became intolerable. The small room was very warm and the smell nauseating but I can still remember that patient. I never again saw such an advanced lesion on the face.

I went to my old school in Croydon as a boarder during those two years, travelling on the overnight sleeper from Inverness to King's Cross 'in the care of the guard'. The headmistress of Croham Hurst came to meet the train at 6.30 in the morning and took me to breakfast in the Station Hotel before driving back to the school, not just the once, but five times in all.

An epidemic of typhoid fever broke out in South Croydon. Even in 1937 it was an uncommon disease and the first cases were not recognised immediately, consequently there was some delay in implementing the essential embargoes on uncooked food and unboiled water. The French mistress fell ill, very ill, and we prayed for her in 'hall' every day.

I was eleven and the oldest in my four-bedded dormitory. One Friday morning Miss Humphrey, the Headmistress, took me on one side and said that a new boarder was being put in my room and I was to be especially kind to her because her mother had just died of typhoid. The school was not a large one and I knew Janet by sight – a plain, spoilt little girl I had always thought and I remember my hypocritical nods of understanding while feeling what a nuisance she was going to be. Janet was six, had no siblings and had never been away from home before. She cried herself to sleep every night and during the day her pathetic blotched face and puffy eyes reminded us all of her grief. I think we sincerely did try our best to comfort her but even we knew that a six year old child should not be sent to a boarding school, however kind and well-meaning, when her mother had just died suddenly and tragically.

We had been told a few days before that the mysterious epidemic was typhoid fever and that there was a strong likelihood that the germs were in the water supply so we were on no account to drink unboiled water or eat anything that had not been cooked. We played games in the afternoon and pelted down the path from the netball court, very hot and sweaty. Rosemary Hart, who had red hair and one of those fair freckled complexions which colour beetroot on exertion, ran straight to the row of basins in the cloakroom, turned on a cold tap and gulped in huge mouthfuls of water. No one else followed her example. She was the only one of my form mates to get the disease but happily both she and the French mistress survived, although they lost most of their hair before it grew in again over the succeeding months.

The epidemic affected nearly 300 people of whom 47 died. The official investigation into its origin found that a workman repairing the water supply pipes at Addiscombe, which supplied all South Croydon, had been too lazy to climb out of the trench to defaecate. He proved to be a typhoid carrier.

I enjoyed my time as a boarder. I was lucky as there were only thirty of us 'in the house' and the staff were unusually child friendly. Quakers had founded the school and many of the staff including the headmistress belonged to the Society of Friends.

I was a great reader and when I was eight my father had introduced me to the mysteries of Sherlock Holmes. I had some trivial complaint and was put in the 'san' for a few days. I was desperately bored and prevailed on the simple under-matron, Mabel, to bring me in some books. She smuggled in two Agatha Christies – *Murder on the Orient Express* and *The Mysterious Affair at Styles*.

I read them surreptitiously and hid them under my mattress, both were quite frightening in different ways but 'Styles' was the worst. There was something very disturbing about the writer of the story being the murderer. Mabel did not come at weekends and Matron made my bed. The offending books were found and were confiscated. I was told that such trash was not suitable reading for the pupils of Croham Hurst. Mabel and I had known we would be in trouble if we were caught. I hope she only suffered a reprimand for her kindness.

The school believed in keeping us up to date with current affairs and sometimes we had guest speakers on contemporary topics. The journalist L.A.G. Strong gave us a talk shortly after Hitler had completed the *Anschluss* in Austria. He unrolled a map of Europe over a standing blackboard in the middle of the hall. The parts occupied by Nazi Germany were coloured in black and, with the annexation of Austria, the 'head' of Czechoslovakia was held in the jaws of Italy and the Reich. He predicted that the invasion of the Czech republic was inevitable, not 'whether' but 'when'. The occupation of the Sudetanland followed in 1938.

Crystal was an Austrian girl of twelve or thirteen, one of us boarders. Hitler was a great favourite of hers and she would persuade the German teacher to let her listen to his speeches on her radio. I can remember Crystal getting very annoyed with the juniors who were amusing themselves in the large common room because we did not treat these opportunities with sufficient respect. I remember his harsh ranting voice, rising to a crescendo followed by a pause and then the voice starting again and continuing relentlessly, much as Charlie Chaplin, several years later, parodied him in the film *The Great Dictator*.

My mother was a great character but she had several mistaken ideas. She wished to perpetuate into adolescence the golden curls I had grown in infancy, regardless of the fact that after every hair washing session my increasingly darkening locks were dead straight. I therefore had my hair done up in 'curly rags' every night of my life and this had to continue when I was at boarding school. The staff had a rota for seeing the younger children into bed and this included dealing with my hair. The rags were strips, usually torn from an old pair of my father's pyjamas, about eight inches long and three wide. In my mother's hands, five were enough to produce the fat ringlets she admired. Miss Humphrey was the best, and Miss Murler, the German mistress was not bad but two or three of the other mistresses were hopeless and Mabel's efforts, which involved using about a dozen very narrow strips, produced a circlet of tight corkscrews like those of Amelia Ann Stiggins, a popular but unladylike character in a children's book of the time. There was always great interest when I appeared at breakfast. If the teachers had been of the betting kind, which they most certainly were not, they would have run a sweepstake on guessing who had done my hair the night before.

When it was decided that I should go back to my old school as a boarder from Aviemore I had to be kitted out with the clothes on the school list. My mother had insisted that, because of the extreme cold of the Highland winters, we should all be put into woollen combinations. I refused to wear them but Mother was equally determined not to waste the good (and expensive) woollen chilprufe 'combies' so she cut off the legs, sewed up the slit at the back and packed them into my trunk. I was an adult before I forgave her for that.

In the autumn of 1938 we moved to Wonersh in affluent rural Surrey south of Guildford. It was a culture shock for all of us, probably for my parents most of all. Our house was in the middle of the village at the meeting of three roads with the Grantley Arms opposite and the village Stores on the other corner. We had an old established garden with mature fruit trees, a vegetable garden, lawn and flowerbeds all enclosed by tall fences concealed by hedges and ensuring privacy. For the first time the consulting room and the waiting room were not inside our own house. Across the drive, but still in the garden, was a sixteenth century weaver's cottage with the built-in wooden beams for the loom still in situ in the smaller of the two downstairs rooms which acted as the waiting room. The other was my father's surgery out of which opened a glorified cupboard which was known to us as 'the bottly room'. I was twelve when we went to live in Wonersh and had been promoted to occasional dispensary assistant for several years. The shelves along one wall held about a dozen large bottles, known as Winchesters, containing a variety of brightly coloured medicines – *mist. tussi rubra* was a particularly rich ruby red, another containing strophanthus and hyoscine was a rather sinister green, while bismuth and kaolin contained a whitish sediment with a supernatant fluid of an unpleasant brown colour.

Most medical (as distinct from surgical) treatment before the war was of the witchdoctor type. Diagnosis was, within the limits of the five senses, relatively accurate but there were few diseases that could be effectively treated – digitalis for heart failure, insulin for diabetes, thyroid extract for myxoedema (thyroid insufficiency), aspirin for rheumatic diseases were available, but nothing could really be done for the killer infections which decimated the young. Streptococcal sore throats, with or without the rash of scarlet fever, often led on to rheumatic fever and subsequent heart disease or to death from nephritis (kidney failure). Tuberculosis was by no means confined to the overcrowded poor; a whole medical speciality and the sanatorium industry were based on its treatment and the segregation of the sufferers. Chronic chest infections were almost the norm in industrial regions and 'winter coughs' the bread and butter of most general practitioners' incomes.

In spite of, almost perhaps because of, this lack of the curative remedies that are available now, people seemed to have great faith in their doctor to help them when they were ill. His (it was very rarely her) personality and manner were essential in establishing the confidence of the patient but even these giants of the past had to have a few stage props. 'The bottle', after the stethoscope, was the most important of these. A cough bottle to cut the phlegm or stomach mixture for indigestion had magical properties and I was fully aware of my privilege in being allowed to participate in the mysteries of making up the medicines in the bottly room. Using a glass funnel my father would pour two ounces of liquid from the appropriate Winchester (large container) into the clear glass medicine bottle marked in ounces up the back.

'Aqua tap to the top,' he would instruct me and I would carefully fill it up to sixteen ounces and then insert a cork of the correct size from the open compartmented tray that sat on the bench top; eight ounce bottles only had one measure of the concentrate.

'Now, I think we'll give Mr Hammond *tussi nigra* this time. He didn't seem to think much of the red cough mixture. Says the black has got the strength.' Once firmly corked the bottle would be laid squarely on a white sheet of paper and one or more labels applied – 'One tablespoon to be taken three times a day after food', 'Shake the bottle' and the paper folded in a particular fashion which resulted in a pleat down the back and a tapering nose of paper at the end with the cork.

I very much enjoyed what came next. A blob of red sealing wax was melted over the flame of a methylated spirit burner and the paper sealed in three places. The patient's name was written on the outside and it was collected from one of the open shelves in the porch outside the waiting room. Each of the surrounding villages had its own shelf to enable the correct bottle to be picked out quickly. Nothing was ever stolen.

Phoney War

The start of World War II was marked by the arrival of coach loads of evacuees from Walworth and round the Elephant and Castle. Mothers and babies were due to arrive first and a billeting officer had conducted a census of all the households in the village to assess their capacity to accommodate these extra bodies. The elderly vicar was a known misogynist who lived in a large Victorian house with a manservant to cater for his needs. The latter was known in our family as the Eunuch on account of his falsetto voice. No woman had ever been known to cross the threshold and now they were compelled to house a slum mum with not one baby but two. Equipment had to be provided and my friend Anne and I walked awkwardly but triumphantly down the village street carrying a child's cot laden with a baby bath, pot, and various bits of appropriate bedding.

I am sure no one realised that cots, baths, and pots were almost certainly unknown in the Walworth Road in 1939. Families crowded into two or three rooms could not afford the space for a baby's cot; baths for adults were made of zinc and hung outside the backdoor when not needed for their weekly purpose and what was the point of a bath for the baby when there was a perfectly good sink to wash him in?

We and our elders were blissfully unaware of the deprivation of much of the population but our intentions were generously meant. Anne and I were proud of the fact that we were now involved in 'war work' and our eagerness to volunteer had not been without the added incentive, as far as I was concerned, of seeing the inside of the vicarage. Our arrival was far from welcome. We had to manoeuvre the cot up the stairs and round a right angle before placing it in a bleak and bare bedroom. The vicar was not to be seen but the Eunuch hovered over us making little yelping noises of anguish as he thought we were going to scratch the pristine white paint on doors and banisters.

Few of the mums and babies lasted longer than a week but the next batch of evacuees were to be of a more permanent order. The children were shepherded into the Memorial Hall and sat frightened and dismayed on rows of wooden chairs, each with a gas mask case and a large label giving their name and home address. The village matrons were gathered round the billeting officer surveying the children much as prospective slave buyers must have viewed the potential of the human goods displayed before them in earlier times.

Eventually all were allocated except for one small boy who was said to be ten but looked no more than seven. The reason nobody had wanted him was only too obvious if one moved near enough. His legs and the backs of his hands had a weeping purulent skin condition, which he scratched frequently, and there was a perceptible odour of dried urine and unwashed clothes about his person. In spite of these disadvantages, or perhaps because he was so used to them that he was unaware, he held his head up bravely and gave a most engaging grin to the Red Cross lady who went over to speak to him.

'Well, Edward,' she said, 'What are we going to do with you?'

'Me nime's not Edward, it's Teddy, Teddy Jaicobs, please Miss.'

The doctor's house had been excluded from the billeting list on the grounds that my mother had more than enough to do running the practice from the house and looking after three children of her own. Now she took charge.

'There's no problem. Teddy will come to us. I'll soon have that little skin problem cleared up and I've some clean clothes that will fit you perfectly,' she said to the child.

How exactly she did it I do not know but in what seemed like no time the scabies and impetigo were gone and he was as clean and healthy as the rest of us. Like several of his Walworth neighbours he also had nits in his hair. They all had their hair shampooed in our garden and then had their heads anointed with oil of sassafras and wound up in a turban of a strip of old sheet. Years later a whiff of sassafras oil brings back a picture of a row of red-eyed children sitting on a red-painted wooden bench in the back garden of the Corner House.

Teddy quickly became one of the family. On Sunday mornings we three children, John my junior by sixteen months, Alison, five years younger, and I, squashed into our parent's bed and enjoyed a cup of tea. Teddy got under the eiderdown and lay across the foot. The bedstead must have been very sturdily built. He was a quick learner although he could barely read because his mother had kept him at home to look after 'the twins'. Her excuse was that he had weak eyes which schoolwork would over-strain and lead to blindness. He moved up two classes in his first term at the primary school in Wonersh. There was nothing wrong with his eyes. At first he would watch to see which implements we used before picking up a spoon or a knife and fork. He had never before sat at a table to eat a meal. It was not long before he demonstrated those entrepreneurial skills that I am sure he would use to great effect when he was older. He made the acquaintance of several of the wealthier local gentry and built up a round of regular small jobs that guaranteed him pocket money. Every Saturday he would go to the Haslams at the Old Mill House and clean their Bentley. In return he was given a very good lunch with the cook and the free run of their large and beautiful garden afterwards. One day I was sent on my bike to bring him home earlier than usual and found him lying on an inflated rubber lilo paddling around the lake in the sun, blissfully happy, king of all he surveyed.

He was scrupulously honest, hard working and as sharp as a needle but after five months my father insisted on another billet being found for him. This was because he believed that my mother was 'overdoing it' and needed some reduction in her workload. We were not supposed to have had an evacuee in the first place. Teddy was placed with a well-to-do couple with an only son and a resident cook who lived in Wonersh Park – an affluent housing development of four (or more) bedroomed houses and large gardens. Teddy lived in the servant's quarters but did not seem to be unhappy. He had grown prodigiously since he came to the country and my mother had supplied his wardrobe from items that my brother had outgrown. Handing down clothes was normal practice even in middle class families, especially as all new clothing was rationed and coupons were precious. The son of the house in his new billet was much of an age with my brother but the lady of the house had little imagination and no knowledge of poverty. When Teddy grew out of his underwear she went into Guildford and bought two pairs of woollen Chilprufe pants and sent the bill to his mother. The cost was probably a third of her husband's weekly wage. She arrived at our house, a raging termagant, short, squat and swarthy in a black skirt and a shiny sateen blouse of a virulent pink, with a disconcerting and very marked squint.

'Why 'as my Edward been moved from your 'ouse? Wasn't 'e good enough for you. . . ' etc etc. My mother was taken aback; she had no idea what Mrs Jacobs was talking about and it took some time and several cups of tea to find out. However the irate woman would not be appeased and she stormed back to London taking Teddy with her. He was ten years old.

One Sunday morning three and a half years later, in the summer of 1943, he arrived unheralded on a skeletal contraption he called a bicycle. It had no saddle and only one ineffective brake. He and his pal had cycled from Walworth (nearly forty miles), leaving at seven a.m. to arrive in Wonersh about four hours later. Ted, as he now preferred to be called, had left school on his fourteenth birthday and was working in a local factory. He gave nearly all his meagre wages to his mother but penny by penny he had saved enough in five months to buy the heap of metal that was his bike. He wrapped rags round the saddle mount and the next Sunday they had set off and here they were. After we had all enjoyed our roast beef and Yorkshire pudding followed by baked rice pudding (how I loved the scrapings from round the dish) we suggested he might like to look round his old haunts.

'No, we'll have to be off.'

'Surely not so soon, you've only just got here?'

'But it'll take us the best part of four hours and we've got to be back before dark 'cos we aint got no lights.'

'And,' chipped in his friend, 'we've got to be at work by ha pas six termorrer.'

The next year he came again, alone this time and on a much better bicycle.

'I got a saddle and new brakes on the old one and a pal of mine sprayed it green. I sold it and got enough to buy this one. Me pal sprayed this one too. It's got gears.' He demonstrated his bright blue machine proudly. Indeed it had gears, more than I enjoyed on my 'sit-up-and-beg' boneshaker. We never saw or heard of Edward Jacobs again but I think he will have been successful in life and hope he is living somewhere in the English countryside he loved so much as a child.

Wonersh in 1939 was still a village. Miss Tippet managed the general store and Mr Pike was the fishmonger. The cobbler, halfway down The Street, was housed in what had been the front downstairs room of an Elizabethan half-timbered house. It was straight from

Beatrix Potter. Mr Brett sat behind a narrow table heightened by a barricade of shoes. He wore a leather apron and held a cobbler's last between his knees while he tapped in the tiny nails needed to keep a new leather sole in place. He was stooped and very bald and when he looked up to greet a customer he pushed his rimless spectacles up onto his hairless pate. The trouble was, that while he was a superb craftsman, he always had too many pairs of shoes to mend and once your shoes were handed over, who knew when you would ever get them back? The tiny space was lined with boots, shoes, sandals and slippers accumulated over the past forty years, mostly covered in dust and cobwebs as the owners had abandoned them decades past.

Brett, as he was known in our house, according to the social usage of the time ('Mr' Brett or his Christian name, which I did not even know, would have been considered very peculiar) was also the verger at the parish church. He would walk solemnly in front of the Reverend Algernon Brown, the vicar, bearing the heavy processional cross, up the aisle to the choir in the presence of a congregation of two or three very elderly ladies. Algy's high church practices were not to the taste of most of the parish. Indeed, we were walked the mile and a half to church in Shamley Green until, eventually, Algy was replaced with a younger Brown, but Brett served the vicar faithfully whatever his churchmanship.

Parts of the village church were very old. The bottom of the tower was pre-conquest with additions in 1180 but the south wall of the nave and much of the west end had been refashioned in the eighteenth century. We had an almost proprietorial feeling for it and delighted in showing visitors its more interesting features. There is a very fine brass of an Elizabethan family, ten boys on one side of the beruffed parents and nine daughters on the other, hidden by the carpet in the lady chapel.

There are two other interesting memorials, one on the north wall of the nave which depicts a single rose stem with the full blown flower head suspended for ever in stone, several inches below the end of the stalk – 'a rose cut off in its bloom'. This records the death of the 26-year-old vicar's wife who died of diphtheria with her newborn infant in 1844. The other is a marble-topped table tomb in the Lady Chapel. The surface has a gloss like polished wax and we all believed the body inside had been embalmed and the preserving oils were permeating the stone. The choirboys dared each other to lick it. We would tell our visitors the tale but did not demand a similar proof of their courage.

The true initiation was the ascent of the bell tower. The privilege of being taken up the tower was not offered to everyone and our parents were, I am certain, completely unaware of what 'going for a stroll round the village with the children' might entail, neither was my sister involved, being so much younger. The key to the door of the ringing chamber was over six inches long and was kept behind one of the beams enclosing the circular wooden staircase up and down which the bell ringers clumped in their boots at the beginning of Matins every Sunday, before slipping out of the side door of the Lady Chapel, their duty done. The light was poor but practice had made me adept at finding the keyhole and turning the heavy lock. The ropes of the six bells hung down through holes in the wooden ceiling some 30 feet above. Access to the bell chamber was by means of a not very robust and nearly vertical ladder. I would go first and push back the trap door, climbing up among the bells, all with their mouths up ready for the next peal. Once there, it was not difficult to balance one's way between them and open the small door onto the narrow walk behind the parapet. The ostensible purpose of this ordeal was to admire the view, and it is true that the top of the church tower is an excellent vantage point from which to survey the surrounding countryside. But the unacknowledged reason was similar to a trial by fire. The ascent of the ladder was not for the fainthearted or those distressed by heights but we were not unkind and only suggested it to those whom we thought could rise to the challenge.

Candidates were not confined to our contemporaries although

I did subject my future husband to the challenge before we became engaged. I knew he did not enjoy ladders but he set his teeth and triumphed, as I had been sure he would. Whether I would have married him if he had chickened out, I do not know. Two better-known friends of my parents survived the experience and even said they appreciated our efforts to entertain them. Sir Philip Gibbs lived in Shamley Green, the next village on the way to Cranleigh. He had been a distinguished war correspondent and was also a well-known and popular novelist. He was in truth a 'gentle knight' whose manner to all was courteous and considerate and who always seemed genuinely interested in the person with whom he was conversing. One day he came to tea when my uncle was staying with us.

'I was always very impressed by how much you managed to observe when you were reporting from the Western Front,' said Uncle Alph. 'How did you do it?'

'Well, some of the time I was in a balloon over the front line.'

'My goodness,' exclaimed Alph. 'You see I was serving as a private, a stretcher bearer, with the Liverpool Scottish in the front line in 1917.'

They were soon engaged in comparing place names and dates. 'I say, listen to this, Lu, Sir Philip was in a balloon overhead at exactly the place and time that I was in the trenches on the ground.'

They were both delighted to have discovered this common bond and Philip Gibbs would ask, 'And how is your Uncle who was in France?' (ie in the Great War) when we met him subsequently.

Sir Philip drove daily into Guildford to catch the train to London and frequently gave a lift to one of his neighbours. Thomas Stearns Eliot was by now living with friends on a nearby estate but still had to work in London for most of the week. Mrs Mirrlees (a Christian Scientist), her spinster sister and Hope, her daughter (a Roman Catholic) and their housekeeper, 'Cocky', who was a Baptist, made a home for 'Tom' for much of the war. My father was their GP and became a friend of T.S. How much my father was aware of his friend's distinction I do not know but my mother was totally out of touch with contemporary literary life. He came to dinner with my parents along with some other friends.

'And would **you** like to write a successful play, Mr Eliot?' she asked him. *Murder in the Cathedral* had been published three years before.

It says much for T.S. that far from cutting us off from his circle of acquaintances he continued to visit and came for afternoon tea on several occasions. On one of these a 'stroll round the village with the children' was suggested and we asked him if he would like to go up the church tower. He accepted with pleasure and survived the test with aplomb. He must have been about 55 at the time. On another occasion we took him swimming in a local lake. He had no swimming gear but we managed to find an old wool bathing dress which, rolled down to the waist over a discarded tie of my father's, served as a pair of trunks. We went to the far end of the rather weedy lake, which still had a pre-war springboard jutting out over the 'deep' end. Each undressing behind a bush, we all enjoyed a swim. T.S. was a breaststroke man, like many of his generation. We all noticed that the moths had been busy in the seat of Aunt Bertha's swimsuit. Whether he observed the holes himself we never knew but, if he did, the knowledge did not spoil his pleasure.

In the early spring of 1944 Mrs Mirrlees invited my father and me to tea. It was a memorable occasion for several reasons. The window seat of the bay widow formed a semi circle round the tea table. Mrs Mirrlees sat in the middle of the bay flanked by Hopey and my father. I perched on one end and Cocky and the spinster aunt sat on chairs to complete the circle. The problems were Mrs Mirrlees' pekes. The two dogs were attached by long leads to their mistress's wrist and were supposed to be lying doggo under the table. Unfortunately they knew there was food above them and were determined to join in the feast. They jumped onto laps, half stood on the table and yapped joyfully while we all tried to field the beautiful bone china plates as they were whisked off the tablecloth by long loops of undisciplined lead. Order was eventually restored and talk turned to the expected invasion of Europe – the long awaited 'second front'.

'Why don't we have a sweepstake on the date?' suggested my father.

'I think that's an excellent idea. Suppose we each put five shillings in the kitty and the guess nearest the day scoops the pool,' said Mrs Mirrlees. The idea was taken up with alacrity and various other persons in the household also contributed their crowns. Tom kept the purse and wrote down our guestimates against our names. I decided on June 3rd, partly because this was my birthday and partly because I genuinely believed the invasion was not going to be as soon as most people thought. Several punters chose dates in the near future, the latest one being for mid-May. Consequently I was a clear winner when Operation Overlord began on June 6th and in due course I was asked back to collect my winnings (£3-15/-) from T.S. Eliot himself. By this time I was sophisticated enough to be aware that he had not only written a successful play but was also a great man in the world of letters.

In 1977 I read a review of a new biography of T.S. Eliot, which dwelt on his aloofness and lack of humour. He had never shown this aspect of his character to us, on the contrary, and I felt I must write to his widow to tell her so. She replied most courteously and said she knew my father's name well as she was working at Faber and Faber as his secretary not long after he left Shamley Green at the end of the war. Her husband does not appear to have told her of his exploits up the church tower or swimming amongst the tadpoles in a moth-eaten bathing suit.

War in Earnest

In May 1940, as the news got worse and worse, my father became increasingly concerned with the imminent possibility of invasion. The doctor in Bramley, half a mile down the road, was also a Scot. He came from Ayrshire and his wife from Thornhill in Dumfriesshire. The two medical expatriates were good-humoured rivals who later became close friends. On one cold wet January day they happened to leave their respective patients simultaneously and walked down the parallel paths from the front doors of adjacent cottages.

After greeting each other Dr Paterson resumed. 'You know Jim, it's poor stuff this flu. There's no more than a couple of visits in it.'

On hearing that the Patersons were going to be evacuated to stay with their relatives in Thornhill, my father looked at a map and decided that Dumfriesshire was as safe as any area could be and still be in touch with civilisation in the form of rail transport and access by road. My mother was very reluctant to leave my father as my parents were close and she knew that life in the south of England was going to be very difficult, invasion or no. Meanwhile as May drew to a close the evidence of disaster was all too apparent.

We went to the local railway station at nearby Shalford and stood on the platform of the 'up' line holding handfuls of two-penny bars of Nestlé's chocolate – these were still available from slot machines in the station at that early stage of the war. The troop trains crawled through, frequently stopping long enough for us to hand out the chocolate to the filthy, hungry and sometimes wounded soldiers who hung out of the windows when the trains slowed through the station. One train halted long enough for me to speak in my halting schoolgirl French to an unshaven and distressed *poilu* (French soldier). He put his hand inside his stained and dirty uniform tunic and brought out his wallet from which he extracted a photograph of a pretty girl of about my age with shoulder length fair hair – his daughter. As the train started to move he tore off the red lapel on his collar, which bore the insignia of his regiment and gave it to me. I have often wondered whether he was eventually reunited with his family. It must have seemed impossible in June 1940.

The next day, June the second, we left by train for London and the North. All the way from Guildford to Waterloo the side of the track was littered with the debris of defeat – discarded socks, single boots, helmets, forage caps and bloodstained bandages. Seeing these must have reinforced my mother's resolve that she was doing the right thing by taking her children away from southern England but her anxiety about her husband's safety must have been acute. If so she kept her thoughts to herself and concentrated on practical matters. I remember a hollow feeling in my gut about the general situation and shut it out of my consciousness whenever I could, but the possibility of defeat never really crossed my mind. I knew and accepted that everyday life might be trying and difficult at times but at that age the future was uncharted and I certainly spent little time worrying about what might happen. Indeed, the experiences of we children for the next five months were never to be forgotten and provided happy reminiscences for the next sixty years.

We lodged for the first few days in the Temperance Hotel in

Thornhill during which time Mother found a cottage to rent in
Penpont, a small village two miles away. 'Salisbury' as it was, and
still is, called, was typically Scottish – sturdily built of stone with a
slate roof, two front rooms on either side of the small hall with a
kitchen behind on one side and a smaller room converted into a
bathroom on the other. The lavatory was on the half-landing and
upstairs were two reasonable bedrooms with a much smaller one
squeezed in between. Before June was out, this little house was
home to nine persons and the focal point for four more.

My birthday, June the third, fell on the first day of our stay in
the Temperance Hotel. I realised that my mother had other things
on her mind but I did not wish the occasion to go unmarked. I had
saved up nearly three pounds and was determined to find
something to give her rather than the other way round. Thornhill
even now is only a large village and did not have a wide range of
shops, but in a side street I found a small dusty window displaying
some very pretty china, a dressing table set decorated with an all
over pattern of small flowers in many colours. I was enchanted
and gathering my courage and my cash I asked how much it was –
pin tray, powder bowl, two candlesticks and a toothbrush holder.

'Three pounds, Miss'

'This is all I've got.' I put a pound note, two ten shilling notes,
three half crowns, two florins and a sixpence on the counter. 'It's
to be a present for my mother, to cheer her up. We've only just got
here from the south and my father's a doctor and so, of course he
had to stay behind.'

Whether it was this heartrending (but true) story or whether
she realised that she was unlikely to find another buyer, she smiled.

'Well, let's call it two pounds ten,' and she picked up all the
money except for one two shilling piece.

I thanked her, probably too much for her native Scots distrust
of effusiveness but I walked out with all my precious china
individually wrapped in sheets of newspaper enclosed in a large
sheet of brown paper tied up with string. My mother was a little

taken aback by the present and did not say much at the time but when we moved into 'Salisbury' at the end of the week the vanity set was carefully laid out on the dressing table and remained with her for the rest of her life.

My Aunt Elsie and my Streatham cousins had even stronger reasons for leaving than we had, as London was already a regular target for German bombers. My Uncle Charlie was also a general practitioner and could not leave, but Ian, much the same age as my brother, had been evacuated with his prep school to Moffat in Dumfriesshire. Elsie followed with Joan, my contemporary, and Sheila, a little younger than my sister Alison. Elsie and Lucy were very old friends. Indeed my parents originally met because the two women nursed together in Edinburgh and so it was both natural and sensible that they should join forces. Hence Salisbury accommodated both families, and, for a time, a school friend of Ian's as well, until by August, his mother arrived from Croydon and rented a small cottage for herself and her three young sons.

Liverpool was also suffering heavy air raids and two more cousins, Paget and Muriel, arrived and were boarded out with a family in the village. Early in August when we were all enjoying a game of 'wavo' (a form of hide-and-seek) up the Scaur burn, we were surprised to see two more children escorted by an adult picking their way through the bracken towards us. As they came nearer I was delighted to see that one was my cousin Pam from the Wirral, but who was the older one? Pam's sister, Pat, was a pretty girl with very blue eyes and two thick fair plats, always full of energy and very good at tennis. This girl seemed tired with her journey and her short lacklustre hair was so thin the she was almost bald in places, but her blue eyes were the same. It was, indeed Pat, but both girls had been ill with typhoid fever and the older sister had been very sick indeed. There were now twelve newcomers in Penpont, sixteen if the Bradley family were included and they usually were. Somehow the village ironmonger found bicycles to fit (more or less) everyone and we cycled en masse all over the countryside in that amazing summer of 1940.

We shocked the Presbyterian sensibilities of the locals by going to church on Sunday mornings (two pews) and then going out all afternoon on expeditions and picnics, swimming in the Scaur pool, climbing the (still) unexcavated fortress of Tynron Doune, cycling to Moniaive and through the grounds of Drumlanrig Castle. The two fathers joined us on holiday for two weeks, but had to forgo any thoughts they might have had of conjugal bliss as they had to stay in The Volunteer Arms along the road.

Soon after Elsie arrived in Penpont it became obvious that she would have to relearn how to ride a bicycle. An iron steed was hired from Willie Mackay and she shakingly mounted with the help of a low wall.

'It's alright Elsie, I've got you, just start pedalling and I'll hold on to the back of the saddle,' said my mother encouragingly.

'Oh, Oh, Lucifer, I can't, I can't, stop, stop,' and she made a series of terrified whoops as she gathered momentum until my mother could no longer keep up with her. I remember we heartless children could hardly stand up we were laughing so much but Elsie triumphed and hardly a day passed without her using it throughout the next five years she spent in Penpont.

When we arrived at the beginning of June we were promptly enrolled into the school at Thornhill that, in Scottish fashion, had only another month of the summer term to run. I joined the four other students who comprised the top class, as I was now fourteen. Jeannie at nearly sixteen, was the oldest pupil in the school. She was not very bright and her employment prospects were poor but her widowed mother received a small allowance as long as she had a child at school. Nan was going on to Dumfries Academy after the summer holidays to continue her education but the two boys were going straight to work on local farms when term ended

The next academic year began in mid-August. Not only had all the final year students left but also the only four in the class below so, when I returned to Wallace Academy, I was actually in a form two years below the one I had started in. This made little practical difference and I was joined by my cousins Joan and Paget while Pat, John, Pam and Muriel were also now on the school roll. My sister, Alison, was very fed up, as she had been taken away from Thornhill in order to look after her younger cousin Sheila, starting school for the first time at the Infants in Penpont.

We three seniors were all studying Latin, as we would need it for school certificate if, and when, we returned to the south. The English mistress, Miss Annie Grant, stayed on after school two afternoons a week and kept us up to the mark. Paget was already doing Virgil but Joan and I were still on *Caesar's Gallic Wars*. I was by far the least competent in this particular field.

None of us had been at a state school before or one that took both boys and girls but we had no problems adjusting. We must have made life for the staff more difficult but also, perhaps, more stimulating and they were scrupulously even-handed in dealing with us when we transgressed. I never had the strap, the thick but pliant leather belt cut at one end into five tails that was vigorously applied to the outstretched palm. If the hand was snatched away two extra strokes were given. John experienced the strap more than once. Certainly the boys were much more likely to be punished in this manner than the girls and most carried a lump of beeswax about the size of a walnut in their pocket as it was claimed that by rubbing it firmly across the palm much of the sting from the strap was removed.

All through those halcyon summer days at Penpont we biked and picnicked, explored and played games in and outside 'Salisbury' while the future of our country was being played out in the skies above the south of England. We knew but did not comprehend. We were worried about our fathers. We listened to the nine o'clock news but it was all so remote it seemed unreal. This was not to last.

One grey November afternoon John and I got off the school bus outside the Volunteer Arms and walked the short distance to Salisbury.

'Children, you have got to be very grown-up and responsible. We are all going home as soon as possible. Now in fact!' Mother had taken John and I into the dining room.

'Why? What do you mean? We can't go just like that,' I expostulated but we could and we did. A telegram had arrived from Dr Paterson. 'Jim ill. Come at once.' We knew it was serious because we had a taxi to take us the fifteen miles to Dumfries to catch the midnight train to London. Alison was sick in the car. The train was already full when it roared puffing and panting into the dark gloom of the station. Mother was squeezed into a packed compartment with Alison on her knee and John had found a corner in another. I spent the night on a soldier's kit bag in the corridor alongside many more weary travellers, most of them in uniform. All the blinds were down because of the black-out and the illumination was minimal. The air was thick with cigarette smoke, sweat and the smell of wet wool and unwashed clothes but the men cheerfully made room for us and did their best to make us as comfortable as possible. We arrived about 7 a.m. in the middle of an air raid. Once again the gravity of our situation was brought home to me because Mother found another taxi to take us nearly forty miles to Wonersh on the far side of Guildford. This time it was John who vomited.

My father was desperately ill with lobar pneumonia and was being nursed in a small three-bedded nursing home run by a close friend. The next day we were taken to see him, the only 'classical case' of this disease I have ever seen until fifty years later, when I was in West Africa.

He was propped up with many pillows, his breath rasped and he could barely speak. Round his mouth were the blisters of herpes and he was temporarily blind, due, it was said, to the effect of M&B 693, the early successor to the first systemic anti-bacterial agent, *prontosil rubra*. Blind or not it saved his life and his sight returned within a few days but the disease resulted in an abscess in his lung, an empyema, for which he had to be admitted to hospital to have it drained with a tube into his chest leading down into a bottle with a water seal hanging under his bed. He eventually recovered and threw himself back, single-handed, into the twenty-four hour demands of rural general practice compounded by the exigencies of war. He toiled from 8.30 in the morning to eight o'clock at night and never knew whether he would be able to sleep the night through without being called out. The doctor in Shamley Green had joined the Navy and his patients had been distributed among the adjacent practices. As a result the area he had to cover had enlarged considerably and driving along narrow country lanes in the minimal light cast by shielded headlamps was a strain in itself. By 1946 his increasing clumsiness and tendency to veer to the right when driving at night were put down to tiredness and reaction to the strain of the past six years but it was not long before he realised that something more sinister was wrong.

The evening before he was due to go into the Royal Surrey County Hospital for investigation for a cerebral tumour he took my arm and we walked along the side of Wonersh Common nearly to Shalford.

'If I have got a brain tumour I will not survive for long and even the tests I am going to have may make me more ill than I am now. I know you will look after your mother. . .' He was not a man who said much about his emotions but that night we came as close as father and daughter could. He was never one to baulk at facing the truth.

In this instance his predictions were half true and he was never able to work again. He had disseminated (multiple) sclerosis and the unsuccessful craniotomy to demonstrate the nonexistent tumour made him a lot worse as did most of the subsequent investigations. His type of MS was the inexorably progressive type. He died peacefully at home of pneumonia nine years later when he was 55.

Our return to Wonersh after the danger-free delights of Dumfriesshire brought us quickly down to earth. London was being bombed nightly and stray German aircraft were relatively common.

I slept on the couch with my head protected by the piano and my brother and sister spent that winter sleeping in the cupboard under the stairs. Apart from a large chunk of plaster falling onto my brother's bed the Corner House suffered no damage but for me it was back to school with a lot of catching up to do after missing the first term of my 'school cert' year.

As the bombing eased off a little the routines of everyday life in time of war became completely normal. We did not question the necessity of carrying our gasmasks in our bicycle baskets or making do with only $\frac{1}{2}$oz of butter a week. We were pleased that we no longer had to wear ghastly felt hats as part of our school uniform and had no problems finding our way round the countryside without signposts using only pre-war maps. Chocolate, oranges and bananas were unknown to small children but sweets were still available and there was no shortage of fruits in their season. The strawberry, plum and blackberry times were all too short but apples and pears kept for months if properly cherished. Parties of fourth formers were organised to pick the Vicar's rose hips to be turned into the Vitamin C rich syrup that was issued gratis to all babies.

We did not remember what it was like to have street lights and no black-out but in the South of England we were very aware of noises in the sky. We could distinguish at once between the sound of German bombers and British fighters and many people, not just the Royal Observer Corps could recognise the silhouettes of most enemy aircraft and the common Allied planes. Our secret worries came from the air, either in the sky or the ether. The wireless dominated lives at home starting with the six p.m. news bulletin. All the gloom and doom was repeated at nine o'clock, this time preceded by the national anthems of all the allies. As one nation after another fell to the Nazis, the anthems of Norway, Denmark Belgium and the Netherlands joined the Marsellaise until late in 1941 our glorious Russian allies joined the cause. By the time the United States joined in, the nine o'clock news started about 8.35, as it had to be preceded by due musical recognition of all our allies.

As there was only enough coal to have one room heated we had to do our homework ('prep' to us) in the sitting room but we became adept at shutting out what we did not want to hear. We had plenty of fun and laughter especially at home. My parents had well-developed senses of humour and on many occasions I can remember laughing so much that it hurt. Some might interpret this as a hysterical reaction to the stresses of our daily lives but it did not feel like that at the time. We all survived the war with our psyches intact and meanwhile village life continued, the basic pattern unchanged even if the trappings had to adapt.

We all relied on the buses. The two Hammond brothers were the drivers and their brother-in-law, Mr Entiknap doubled up as driver or conductor, but it was Mrs Entiknap the conductress, who remains vivid in the memory.

'All turn round and face the driver please.' This ensured that not an inch of space was wasted. There were often more standing than sitting and Mrs E would hang on to the vertical pole on the open platform, her feet just on the edge and her slim angular body swaying about as the grossly overloaded little bus would take the corners and pant along the straight. One Saturday as her husband drove the bus along the flat stretch towards the bridge over the river he slowed to a crawl so that his wife, hanging on to the pole by one arm and leaning out from the platform could call out to their one ewe lamb as he was fishing from the bank

'Gay, you go back home now. It's dangerous.'

Gay was a singularly inappropriate name for the unfortunate boy at that stage of his life as he was as rotund as the original eleven-year-old Bunter from Greystoke while his parents were as thin and spare as is compatible with health.

The Brown buses never let us down. The Hammonds and Entiknaps provided a seven day and evening service for the six long years of war. They probably suffered from chronic fatigue as did most adults during that time but the buses never missed a day's work and grumbles concerned the weather not their health.

'Cutting Chapel Like Me?'

I had always wanted to be a doctor and so had no difficulty in deciding what subjects I needed to study once I matriculated with the necessary grades. It was passing the First MB, the preliminary examination in basic science subjects – chemistry, physics and biology for the University of London degree in medicine and surgery – MB BS, that was a major hurdle. In the end it was the flying bombs that saved my medical career from disaster before it had even started. My first attempt was made from school. There were no problems with zoology and botany (combined in biology), the teacher was excellent and I already had a 'credit' in school certificate biology but I knew nothing of chemistry or physics. Miss Morrison was not the one to help me make up the deficit. She would perch her five foot nothing on a stool in the chemistry/biology/physics lab (there was only one) and spend most of our lessons gossiping about other members of the staff. She it was who told us that 'Grumbo' (English) had married a Free French private and subsequently let slip that that was why Madam Bizet (French, of course) was knitting little white garments. We shared her genuine grief when Grumbo lost the baby, but it was no surprise when I failed my first MB physics. It is obvious now that poor Morry was out of her depth.

She had had almost no experience of teaching science above school certificate level but the war had made girls think seriously about their careers unless they wanted to join one of the women's services. The less academic did, but the rest of us hoped to go to university and it was largely the science subjects that delayed conscription. The school was faced with providing for the needs of six or eight girls wanting to read agriculture, dentistry, pharmacy and medicine.

We were divided into 'Houses' and Merriman's housemistress was an already embittered music teacher in early middle age who ran a project breeding rabbits. This was ostensibly to supplement the meat ration but, as a spin-off, she informed me, as the Head of House, 'that it would help to teach the facts of life to the middle school.' I privately thought that Daisy Mann and June Allan could probably teach her many more sophisticated facts than they would learn from observing the copulations of rabbits especially as the animals frequently seemed unaware of the sex of their partner and sometimes made amatory advances to the wrong end.

'Now, Elizabeth, I am putting you in charge of the rabbits – you must make a rota for feeding, cleaning them out and so on and as you are a day girl and live so near, you will be able to carry on through the holidays. Remember, it's all part of our war effort,' she added when she noticed that I was about to protest.

So, I had been saddled with the rabbits. One evening about six thirty I was fetching my bicycle after I had checked that they had been shut up for the night, when I caught sight of a shadowy figure at the other end of the shed.

'Who is it?' I called out

'It's only me.' To my surprise Morry emerged onto the drive, wheeling her bike.

'Oh, it's you, Miss Morrison. Cutting chapel like me tonight?'

'Well, not exactly. I'm just going off to Shalford to do my evening shift at the fibre works.'

'How often do you do that?'

'Four nights a week. It's only for three hours – seven until ten. I'm back in school by twenty past usually.'

'But what do you do there?' I asked, thinking she was probably helping in the canteen as most of us did in the NAAFI in Guildford at the weekends.

'Well we're not supposed to say really, but actually they make spare reserve tanks for Spitfires and I cut the shapes out of the fibre sheeting.'

My respect for Morry took a quantum leap. To cycle two miles through the winter dark and wet to work at a physically demanding manual job after teaching all day required dedication not demonstrated by many. Unfortunately respect and even affection did not improve her teaching skills and I duly left school and went to the 'Tech' – Guildford Technical College.

External candidates for the First MB had to sit the exam in London. This entailed going to stay with my aunt and uncle in Purley on the outskirts of the city, and going up to 'town' with the bowler-hatted city businessmen by train, three mornings in a row. Each subject consisted of a three-hour paper and a practical exam. Although I had only failed in physics I had to resit all three subjects. It was the winter of 1944 and the onslaught of 'doodle bugs' (flying bombs or V1s) was at its height. They were terrifying to observe, and even more to hear; their squat cigar-shaped bodies with stumpy wings emitted a tail of fire and black smoke with a noise like a runaway steam engine. Flying at 1500 feet they were easy to see but it was the noise that attracted attention. As long as it was audible, the fear was relatively dormant. It was when it stopped that internal panic took over. When the fuel ran out, designed to happen somewhere over London, the engine cut and the missile began its fifteen-second downward glide to earth. A doodlebug overhead was nothing to fear even if it stopped, it did not fall vertically out of the sky. One knew that someone else's 'name was on it' and this time we were safe. Many fell in Kent, far short of their target, part of which was known as 'Doodle Bug Alley', but a fair number landed in our part of Surrey. I was familiar with the approaching roar and the horrifying silence while one counted fifteen seconds before the inevitable explosion.

In its wisdom, the University of London arranged for some of the external students to sit the First MB examination in three classrooms on the top floor of, I think, the North London Polytechnic near The Angel, Islington. We sat at old-fashioned school desks with a stern-faced male invigilator. After half an hour or so we heard the air-raid siren rising and falling like a monstrous aural scenic railway but we were used to its stomach-churning ululations and continued to write. Very soon afterwards there were repeated short sharp whistles from immediately above our heads. There was obviously someone on the flat roof keeping an eye on the sky. At this point we heard a long rumble from the classroom next door as the candidates got off their chairs and crouched down with their heads under their desks. As the rumble died away we could hear the approaching flying bomb. We continued to sit and pretended to write, squinting up at our invigilator who made no sign that he was even aware of it. The noise increased until the roar crescendoed overhead and two or three minutes later stopped. We silently counted and then heard the crump drowning the sound of the students next door resuming their seats.

Fortunately for me this potential distraction occurred several times during the course of the morning. I believe we were all given bonus marks as a result, whether we were among the stiff upper lip set or those supervised by the less stoical lady supervisor in the next room.

I began my life as a medical student of King's College in the Strand in January 1945. By that time the flying bombs had been replaced by V2s or rockets, which were more devastating and arrived without warning. We were in the biochemistry lab about noon one day when there was a tremendous explosion and we all ducked down under the marble-topped benches. Amazingly only one window cracked and rather self-consciously we stood up and went on with our experiments. We could see an expanding cloud of blackness mushrooming above the buildings in the direction of Fleet Street. At lunchtime, my friend Paula and I determined to see if we could find out where the rocket had fallen and set out down the Strand in an easterly direction. We continued down Fleet Street and then north up Fetter Lane to Holborn and walked up onto Holborn Viaduct. Immediately to the north the ground below us was totally devastated. We were looking down on what had been Smithfield Market. Buildings, roads, stalls, lanes, people had all been reduced to a mishmash of wooden slivers superimposed on unidentifiable debris. We could taste the dust that was still rising from the ruins. We had seen bomb damage before but never to this extent and never so soon after it had happened.

I had two great friends at school, Paula and Anne. Paula had a small heart-shaped face, snub nose, huge blue eyes with correspondingly luscious lashes and a flawless pink and white complexion. She had a neat waist, well but not over-developed bosom and a superb pair of legs. She was in fact highly desirable. How much she was aware of her attractions I do not know but, at the Tech, she had only to bend her willowy neck round the door of our tutor's office and say 'Mr Llewellyn. . .' and he was on his feet ready to sort out her problem. He would be rewarded by a slight flutter of the eyelashes over those wonderful blue eyes and he was all attention. She was not really a flirt, just extremely attractive and naturally the men (and boys) responded. I was not jealous. The rest of us just accepted that Paula was the pretty one.

Anne, slim but flatter, had a 'nice' face. I suppose really she was rather plain and she did remind one of a friendly pony but she had a warm, welcoming expression and always saw the best in every-one, however much of a scumbag the rest of us knew them to be.

I was somewhere between these two extremes, quite pretty (but with rather unemphatic eyebrows) reasonable figure but almost no waist and thickish legs. We were all three good at lacrosse and reasonably intelligent and came from very similar middle class professional backgrounds. Anne went off to the all-female Royal Free Medical School while Paula and I were still at the Tech. In spite of her unisex education Anne was the first to find her lifelong helpmeet and got married while she was still a student. She had four months leave of absence to enable her to adjust to the difficulties of being a married woman (the Royal Free policy at that time) and then resumed her clinical studies and duly qualified. She continued to practice medicine to which she dedicated her time and effort, especially working with the young chronic sick for which thirty years later, she was honoured with an OBE. She and her husband had no children of their own but for over fifty years their house was, and is, a home and refuge for countless lonely souls and lame ducks as well as being a focus for both their warm closely linked families.

Paula was over thirty before she found her permanent partner. Medicine never meant the same to her as it did to me. The geographical and social constraints imposed on her by marriage left only a little time for minimal part-time sessional work and, with a demanding husband and three boys, she did her best to be content.

There were several young men who haunted me in my late teens. Geoffrey was at least ten years older and had a permanently damaged heart from rheumatic fever. He had coached Anne in physics prior to her acceptance by the London School of Medicine for Women (Royal Free) and organised a boating trip on the Norfolk Broads. My parents met Captain and Mrs Tottenham to decide whether they could allow their daughters (aged 18 and 19) to join the party! We had a great holiday but the idea that any of us would even want to 'carry on' with Geoffrey (weak heart), Kenneth (deformed arm) or Chris (sixteen year old schoolboy) never crossed our minds. I was presented with an album of very good photographs at Christmas and went out with Geoffrey a few times subsequently.

By that time I was living in London and I confess to a rather malicious delight in teasing him – not by flirting but by causing him embarrassment. He was a real prude and blushed at any reference to anything of a sexual nature. Once we went for a row on the Thames and there were so many used condoms in the river that every time he brought the oars out of the water they were festooned with johnny bags. On another occasion we went downriver to where a frigate was moored and open to the public. Once on board there was no escape until the next tender came to pick us up an hour later. There were copulating couples round every corner, and there are many corners on a naval vessel. Most were standing up I was interested to notice as, until then, I had assumed that a horizontal position was necessary. Poor Geoffrey, that was the last time he asked me out.

George was working for first MB at the Tech as I was. I liked him very much and we went out together quite frequently. He went on to Barts (St Bartholomew's Hospital Medical College) which was evacuated to Cambridge and he invited me to a May Ball during the time he was there. I did not possess a 'ball' dress and clothes coupons were in very short supply. My mother found a pair of blue tapestry curtains with an all-over pattern of small sprigs of flowers in pink and gold. It was really very pretty and the local village dressmaker made it up into a full-length gown with a fitted bodice and full skirt. I was very pleased with it and was flabbergasted at George's reaction when he ceremonially helped me off with my coat. He was far from pleased and it took me a few minutes to find out why. It was the fitted bodice – too fitted, too flattening. George was definitely a boobs man but I had not realised it. On another occasion he took me down to Beachy Head in his underpowered and unreliable old banger. It was a scorching day and the sun reflected relentlessly off the sea. On the way back we stopped at a suitably lonely spot and kissed. His technique lacked finesse and I am sure he had had little practice and neither had I – no tongues, just pressure, repeated pressure.

I was duly returned to the Mayday Hospital in Croydon where I was doing two weeks midwifery. The next day I had the most extensive labial herpes (cold sore) that I have ever seen. My lips were swollen and there was an extensive area of blisters round my mouth. Trauma plus a double dose of ultra violet from sky and sea had done their worst. I knew if my lesions were suspected by those in authority, I would be banned from the delivery room, so I wore a mask all the time I was in the wards or the labour suite. It was an uncomfortable price to pay in the unusually hot weather, especially as I had not really enjoyed the experience.

The trouble was that George had THICK LIPS. I found them a total turn-off. I would have liked to have fallen in love with George but I knew it would never happen. I never told him (how could I?) that this was why our relationship never went farther than friendship but his mother never forgave me. When, eventually, I became engaged to someone else, she went to see my parents (they had never met her) and harangued them about my duplicity in leading on her ewe lamb. Happily he married an extremely pleasant and eminently suitable girl and became a much respected (but always a little pompous) GP.

Once I became a second year medical student at King's College in the Strand the disproportion between the numbers of men and women increased the possibilities, but strange as it must seem to modern youth we were not really interested. Of course there was a little mild flirting and badinage but developing 'a relationship' with one of our fellow students was not something we took seriously. We had little time for extra-curricular activities.

After a term with Paula in the house within Lambeth Hospital where her father was the Medical Superintendent, I moved to 'digs' (lodgings) in Streatham along with two other students. My father gave me £200 per annum for three years, all he could afford. The University of London charged £50 a year for my medical education.

My landlady demanded £2 10/- per week and my tram fare from Streatham to the Strand was four pence each way. It was quicker to go by bus but this cost an extra penny on each fare and I needed those ten pence to balance my weekly budget. Lunch was a cup of coffee and a cheese roll for 1/3d in the 'Creamery' next door to the college. Most of us were in the same boat and the few who weren't were wise enough to disguise their relative affluence.

One of our fellow students was Doreen St Davids who alternated her lunch date with her husband between the Creamery and the House of Lords. She had a peculiarly penetrating voice with a gratingly upper class accent tinged with an Australian twang but she was quite without pretension. 'See you at the House tomorrow, Jestyn,' would cut through the general babble and heads would briefly turn. Nobody would guess seeing her tall rather angular figure in the dowdy tweed coat with its undulating hem partially held up by safety pins that she was a viscountess and the mother of four children.

The women student's locker room was small and had a characteristic pungent odour, a mixture of formalin and human body fat which impregnated our lab coats, with overtones of female sweat, odorono (the universal deodorant) and sometimes, as an antidote, a cigarette. It was on the top floor close to the anatomy department where we spent a great deal of our time, dissecting. Each corpse provided material for twenty students, three to each arm and leg, four for the head and neck and four for chest and abdomen. The novices started on a limb and painstakingly traced out the course of the cutaneous nerves before being allowed to penetrate the deeper layers exposing the nerves, blood vessels, muscles and joints. The origin and insertion of every muscle in the body had to be learnt by heart.

'The middle third of the superior nuchal line and the external occipital protruberance. . .' comes unbidden into my mind. While this almost useless task was being performed one had the opportunity to set the world to rights and to enjoy the company of our seniors who were discovering the intricacies of the head and torso that would have a great deal more relevance to our future studies. We certainly improved our manual dexterity while carving up the dead and learnt a lot more than anatomy in the dissecting room.

I did acquire one devotee while I was in the Strand. Thomas lived with his parents somewhere near Greenwich. He would contrive to accompany me on my bus ride back to Streatham, which was ninety degrees out of his way, but he had an encyclopaedic knowledge of the Southern Railway timetable. By means of inter-connections via London Bridge he would justify lengthy diversions on his way home for the pleasure of my company. The trouble was that he was so boring and the fifty-minute journey felt like a hundred and fifty before I could escape.

Each of the five floors in the medical block had a long central corridor with a staircase at either end. Many a time I pelted down the stairs and saw Thomas turn the corner at the opposite end. Once at ground level I could either go out into the Strand or dive down into the huge tunnel that ran underneath the college quadrangle carrying the trams from Kingsway to the Embankment. This was my preferred route because, with any luck, I could catch the Streatham tram and go home in peace. Sometimes I hid behind a pillar until I had seen him disconsolately move off to catch his normal train.

He was a sensitive young man and took fancied slights very much to heart even when I had no idea that I had upset him. He eventually realised that I was never going to take him seriously and ended his advances with a dramatic letter in which he called me, amongst other things, 'a black-hearted Jezebel'. He was always rather hot on scriptural references.

Married Bliss

I went home to Wonersh about once a month, being a member of the university lacrosse team. My fare to the ground at Motspur Park was subsidised and by means of a series of buses I could reach home for less than two shillings. I had hardly arrived one Saturday evening when I had a phone call from my aunt in Streatham. For Elsie to make a toll call meant serious business, and so it proved, although at the time I had no idea of its ultimate importance.

'Libs dear, would you come back tomorrow in the morning? I want you to come to tea and help me entertain this very difficult young man.'

'What difficult young man?'

'Well, he's Cedric's brother.' Cedric was the name of my cousin Joan's boyfriend in Edinburgh where they were both medical students.

'He's come back from the war with a terrific chip on his shoulder and now he's got this job in London. Joan says he doesn't know anybody and wants me to ask him out to Streatham.'

I was not all that keen to cut my weekend short but reluctantly agreed and duly presented myself at 34 Tooting Bec Gardens at 3.30 the next day.

The end result was that I married Graham two years later and we had twenty eight happy and not unproductive years together. He had graduated from Edinburgh in 1940, winning the Ettles Scholarship and gold medal for his year. He then served for six years in the RAF, initially with fighter squadrons in the south of England and then in North Africa, Italy, Iraq and Egypt, during which time he passed the London MRCP exam when he was home on leave. On returning to his native city at the end of the war, he found the academic posts filled by those who had been demobbed before him. He would have been unemployed if it had not been for the generosity of the Professor of Pathology, Murray Drennan, who gave him a post as a demonstrator and a small place in his lab to carry out research.

A year later he became a research fellow in Professor George Pickering's unit at St Mary's Hospital in London. Hence my aunt's SOS.

It was no wonder he felt hard done by when, at the age of thirty after such a brilliant start, he was earning £400 p.a. on the bottom rung of the academic ladder. He soon realised that it was the best thing that could have happened to him. Pickering was a superb teacher and had an international reputation for research. This was the real start that Graham needed to stimulate his enquiring mind and foster his life-long interest in clinical research.

Our courtship was carried out in the bitter winters and postwar restrictions of impoverished life in London in the late 1940s. I would go to Oxford and Cambridge Mansions in Paddington at the end of my day's study at King's College Hospital in Camberwell and he would cook us a boiled egg each, sent by his mother from Edinburgh every week. We never ate out. We could not afford it. Then back to the lab in the basement at St Mary's where he was experimenting on blood pressure in rabbits whose intravenous infusions needed changing every eight hours. This did not leave long for courtship and the lab was far from salubrious, especially when one could see through the grimy glass at the top of the windows the unsteady feet of the prostitutes cramped into their 'winkle pickers' as they walked up and down their 'pitches' in Praed Street.

During an interval between parts of my final MB BS exam I visited the formidable lady doctor who had briefly instructed us in the practical aspects of venereology; women students only, women patients only, any man was *verboten*. She also invited us, two at a time, to be observers at an evening session of the North Kensington Women's Welfare Clinic, which provided one of the few contraceptive services in London at that time. Diaphragms were the order of the day (or night) and as these were the only contraceptive appliances that worked, apart from the ubiquitous durex, which were conventionally associated with preventing men from being infected by prostitutes, their use was promoted with almost missionary zeal.

They were all that women could use themselves to control their fertility. Unfortunately, as I was to find out, they were not as efficacious as their advocates believed. Nevertheless caps were all we had and I duly presented myself at Dr Hammant's consulting room somewhere near Harley Street. She fitted me with a Dutch cap. As I had been using tampons for some time this was not a difficult procedure but I found it extraordinarily tricky trying to insert it myself.

'You'll find you get the hang of it once you're on your own at home and have a bit of practice.'

I dressed and somewhat awkwardly opened my handbag.

'Don't worry about that. We're all members of the same profession,' the Doctor said. She added gruffly, 'Don't be too disappointed if it's a bit of a disaster the first time.' It was good advice and I subsequently passed it on sometimes to other nervous young maidens in similar circumstances.

I graduated at the end of October 1949 and was married two weeks later in Wonersh Church by my much-revered mentor Canon

Hughes of Southwark who subsequently became the Bishop of Croydon. Graham and I spent the first week of our honeymoon in the New Forest and the second in Lyme Regis where my principal memory is of being perpetually hungry. The genteel private hotel was used to catering for elderly residents whose appetites matched the miniscule portions on our plates. On December 1st I started as a house physician at King's College Hospital. At least that was the official description but in reality I was living in Dulwich Hospital where KCH had an outpost of empire.

Graham moved up to Sheffield as a lecturer in the Department of Pharmacology and Therapeutics in January 1950. We had two nights together over a short weekend during the next five months. The only time I left Dulwich Hospital was to go on the tram over the hill twice a week to outpatients at King's. Like all my fellow housemen and women I was on call all day and all night, week in week out but because there was so little we could do about most medical emergencies I was not often called out of bed, unlike my fellow residents in surgery. Because it was so difficult to contact me, I was only called for true emergencies. Although Dulwich Hospital had women residents, I was the only junior female on the King's staff and there was no accommodation available. I was housed in the nurse's home of St Francis Hospital next door. Extensive grounds surrounded both hospitals but the only physical connection between them was a long dark tunnel under a railway line. St Francis was a psychiatric hospital at that time and was reputed to house potentially raving lunatics, so no student nurse was allowed to go through the tunnel alone. Ward Sisters, those of senior rank and newly qualified female doctors were supposed to be robust enough to defend themselves if an emergency arose (and it never did as far as I am aware).

A few days after I started my residency a woman was admitted suffering from a rare disease, familial telengiactasia. This results in multiple collections of superficial blood vessels developing in the skin but, more lethally, also in the mucous membranes. These bleed

very easily and profusely. Direct pressure soon arrests the haemorrhage but lesions in the nose and at the back of the throat are very
difficult to control and she had already been admitted seven times
for blood transfusions and control of the bleeding area. She told
me she slept with a bucket beside her bed, the blood loss was so
heavy and unpredictable. She was convalescent from the most
recent attack and had had three pints of blood transfused and a
lesion in the back of her nose cauterised and was looking forward
to going home. That night she started bleeding again. The night
sister called the gate porter to phone for the ENT resident and also
for me as the patient was certainly going to need more blood. The
porter tried to get through to his opposite number at St Francis
but in those days all telephone exchanges were manual and the
two hospitals, although only separated by a railway line were in
two different exchange zones. It was not unusual to have difficulties
raising the operator and after five futile minutes he called back to
the ward and said he could not get through. Night Sister was in
charge of six wards, including the one with the exsanguinated
woman, but she was not allowed to send a more junior nurse to
fetch me (in case she was molested by a madman in the tunnel)
and she had to leave the patient and the rest of her charges while
she ran through the darkness to the nurses home on the other side
of the track. Traditionally nurses are only allowed to run in cases
of haemorrhage or fire. I think I must have gone to sleep subconsc-
iously expecting a crisis because I am sure I heard her running
footsteps on the linoleum of the corridor before she knocked on
my door.

'Come as quickly as you can Dr Wilson, it's Mrs Follett and
she's bleeding again,' she breathlessly whispered and was gone at
once back to her post.

I scrambled into the minimum of clothes and ran into the dark
night trying to think what I was going to have to do. The patient's
blood group was known but it had to be 'cross matched' with that
intended for the transfusion as the science of haematology was

still primitive. We knew of A, B, AB, and O. The 'Rhesus Factor' had been discovered in 1938 but the finer differences between blood groups were still a mystery. We knew that transfusing someone with blood, even of the same group and Rh factor could sometimes result in disastrous reactions. Hence the need for cross matching. In theory I knew how to do this but in practice this would be the first time.

I reached the ward, two floors up, Sister met me and we walked together to the dimly lit bedside. Mrs Follett looked up and I knew she recognised me. She was very pale and sweat was beading on her forehead, which a nurse was gently wiping away as it formed. Her nostrils were packed with thin cotton bandage, already blood stained and the young ENT houseman had sent for his registrar knowing the problem was beyond his skills.

'Have we got any Group A Rhesus positive blood?' I asked.

'No, you'll have to go to maternity and borrow some from them. Tell them we'll replace it tomorrow from KCH.'

'Where is Maternity?' I asked. I had only been in the hospital three days and was ignorant of most of its geography outside my own immediate orbit.

Having received directions I hurried off to the other end of the hospital to beg and borrow at least two pints of A positive blood. It was two o'clock in the morning and the midwife in the labour ward was having a cup of tea between deliveries. She was very reluctant to hand over the bottles – blood came in bottles in those days – and they were very cold, taken straight from the huge maternity ward refrigerator. I put one in each pocket of my white coat and ascended once more to D2. I knew I had to go to the pathology lab to do the crossmatching myself but I had no idea where it was.

'It's on the top floor, under the roof but you have to get the key from the gate porter as it's locked at night.'

Downstairs again, the bottles heavy in my pockets, and outside to the gatehouse.

'Please can I have the key to the path lab?'

The man got up and handed me an ordinary-looking door key from a row of hooks on the wall with a dirty label attached to it by an old bit of string 'Path Lab'.

I hurried up four flights to the door of the lab, inserted the key and was quite unable to turn it. I rather pride myself on my strong wrists and my hands are too big for a real lady but I could not turn that key. By this time I was becoming very anxious. I could feel the panic rising and had to make a great effort to control it. I left the blood bottles on the floor outside the door and went back to the porter.'

I'm awfully sorry but I just can't turn the key. I'm afraid you'll have to come and help me.'

His look said it all.

'That's what comes of having women on the house,' (ie, as residents) he grumbled aloud.

'I'm not supposed to leave the switchboard. It's not my job in any case. You'll have to get somebody else'

'Who? There is nobody else and while we stand arguing the patient is dying.' He reluctantly gave way and toiled up to the fourth floor – an exertion which probably influenced his initial reluctance as much as his job description. He unlocked the door and I was left alone in this cluttered laboratory, lit, in daylight by skylights, but now by a miserable forty-watt bulb. This lab was used for all the pathology services in the hospital and I had first to locate the haematology bench. Once there I saw an untidy collection of old porcelain plates, rectangular and each containing a dozen thumbprint impressions in which the bloods could be mixed. A drop of the patient's blood had to be pipetted onto the plate and then a drop of the to be transfused blood. They should be mixed together with the end of the pipette and carefully observed for two minutes. If the blood started clumping the two were incompatible but if there was no reaction, all was well.

I was pretty distraught by this time and the light was poor but I was certain no reaction had happened with either bottle and,

without waiting to clear up after myself, I ran downstairs to the
ward. I had been away about twenty minutes and Mrs Follett was
visibly worse although the ENT registrar had managed to stop the
haemorrhage from the back of her nose. The only light was from a
low wattage bulb over sister's desk in the middle of the ward. Individual bed lamps were unknown, as were curtains. Two inadequate
screens obscured what was happening from any other patient awake
and curious enough to watch. I extended the patient's arm and
looked for a vein, wrapped a sphygmomanometer cuff round her
upper arm and inflated it. Her blood pressure was almost
unrecordable and the sustained pressure did not result in a visible
vein.

The ENT registrar said, 'You'll have to cut down on an ankle
vein. They've all collapsed because she has lost so much blood.'

I must have looked at him in desperation.

'Would you like me to give it a go first?' he said.

'Oh, would you? I've never done it before.' I was so relieved I
almost wept but stiff upper lip won the day and the transfusions
were duly given.

I wish I could say that this story had a happy ending, that it did
not was probably my fault. The next morning Mrs Follett was feeling
much better and was even able to drink her breakfast tea but as the
day wore on she developed a fever. Her temperature went up and
continued to rise, 104, 105, 106. She had several rigors, shivering
attacks associated with fever, and became delirious. The consultant
arrived, a kindly man who ordered redoubling of the icepacks and
other nursing measures which were being used to try and bring
down the fever. She was given injections of penicillin, the only
antibiotic we had, in case she had septicaemia, but all to no avail.
When her temperature reached 108 she died. The death certificate
said 'malignant hyperthermia', 'pre-existing condition Familial
telengiectasia'.

A week or so later when I was attending outpatients I overheard
my chief discussing the case with the senior registrar

'Extraordinary case that. Never seen one like it before but, in my own mind, I'm sure it was a transfusion reaction. The bloods were incompatible but I don't want young Dr Wilson to realise that. I'm sure she did her best in very difficult circumstances.'

'Yes, you're right there. If the patient had been in King's, where she had always been admitted before, there would have been a resident pathologist who would have sorted out the blood and it wouldn't have been left to a newly qualified houseman. I went up to the Dulwich lab myself after the patient died and it was an absolute shambles, even in the day. What it was like at night with no-one to check the findings must have been a nightmare.'

'Yes, well, I don't want her to feel that she has a patient's death on her conscience at the start of her career. The poor lady could not have survived many more of those bleeds in any case.'

I never let on that I had overheard this conversation but I have never forgotten it, nor Mrs Follett's death and I am still not sure whether it really was my wrong reading of the cross matching which caused it. I know I thought at the time that I had got it right.

In the last week of my residency the registrar noticed something amiss.

'Are you all right Libby?'

'Oh, yes, I'm fine.'

'Well you don't look it. Let me take your temperature.' In those days doctors still carried thermometers and could read them.

'101. Not fine.'

I was warded and diagnosed as having glandular fever. After another week convalescing, I travelled up to Sheffield and connubial bliss. The first few nights in the boarding house were far from blissful but we were fortunate in being shortlisted from over two hundred applicants for a pleasant one-bedroomed flat. The rent was five guineas a week and Graham's salary only £600 a year but, like all the other young postwar couples, we desperately wanted a PLACE OF OUR OWN. So real married life began in 41A Ashland Road, Netheredge in Sheffield in July 1950.

A Voracious Husband

My visit to Dr Hammant's consulting room began my long association with family planning and my intimate knowledge of its pitfalls was demonstrated almost immediately. Our eldest daughter was born in March of the following year. The midwife's 'It's a girl and she's just perfect' were music to my ears. Throughout the pregnancy I had been secretly worried in case her conception when I was convalescent from glandular fever, might have resulted in some congenital abnormality. I found out much later that Graham had had the same fear but we had both kept our anxieties to ourselves so that the other would not worry.

So began my obstetric history, short in time but long in experience. My last pregnancy resulted in the birth of our youngest daughter on July 30th 1959 and in between the first and the last I had five full-term deliveries and a miscarriage; nine pregnancies in eight years, wonderfully ironic for a family planning doctor. I enjoyed neither pregnancy nor childbirth and can only assume that women who say they have never felt better than when they were pregnant must enjoy a very miserable state of health for most of their time on this earth. I soon found that 'morning sickness' was a euphemism invented by those past childbearing who gave false messages of hope while privately rejoicing that it was now another generation's turn to experience the wretched side effects of pregnancy. 'Morning, noon, and night' sickness was the reality for me and, far from ending at three months, it only gradually petered out when my vastly increasing girth presented other unpleasant symptoms.

I vomited unpredictably and precipitately well into the fifth month. I was working in the mornings as a casualty officer at the Sheffield Royal Hospital and more than once had to get off the bus before I reached my home stop, to be sick into the gutter at the roadside.

Almost worse than the vomiting was the involuntary stress incontinence which accompanied each violent contraction of my diaphragm. I had to carry a spare pair of pants in my handbag wherever I went. Even wearing a sanitary towel was insufficient protection if my bladder was more than half full. I had to plan my life from hour to hour to avoid the awful embarrassment of publicly losing control over both ends at once. Although I was never so sick again as I was with that first pregnancy I continued to feel nauseated and sometimes to throw up if I became very tired throughout the next seven pregnancies. I had never suffered from motion sickness but I soon realised that feeling sick when a passenger in a car was, for me, an infallible sign of early pregnancy.

One weekend in October in 1958 we were driving to Lincoln to show an American visitor the glories of the cathedral. As we drove through the flat bedraggled fields of the fens with the great church on its hill in the distance dominating the landscape, I said, 'Please will you stop the car Graham?' I will never forget the look he gave me, horror and despair succeeded by resignation. He knew exactly what it meant.

We had left Richard the baby, and Rosemary, who was barely 15 months, with Mrs Faxon, our mother's help. She was happy to look after them for the day and there was not enough room in the Vauxhall to accommodate the carrycot and the toddler and the three other children, (seven, six and three) in addition to the three adults. In those days we had no worries about children travelling in the front on someone's knee or squashed into the back in a double layer of hot humanity. To both of us the thought of yet another infant was appalling but we had to accept it. We had no other option.

Through out these pregnant years I continued to work, part time but with little maternity leave – two weeks before the Expected Date of Delivery, and four afterwards. I had no resident help but Mrs Faxon arrived every morning at nine and became part of the family for twelve happy years. She overlapped for an hour with Nanny Mitch who came at 1.30. Sometimes we would all pile into the landrover, by that time the only vehicle which could accommodate the whole family, and go on an expedition to Bellevue Zoo in Manchester or some nearer Site of Special Interest for Children. One day we went to Treak Cliff Cavern in the Peak District. We parked the vehicle and got out.

'Margaret, you and John hold Poodle's hands.' Poor Penelope, her mass of short curls condemned her to this nickname until well after she started school.

'I'll carry Richard because he is the heaviest and Mrs Faxon can take Rosie as she can walk if it's not too far. Nanny Mitch do you think you can carry Die?' Fortunately the youngest was a neat little baby, not yet a year old and hopefully not too much for Nanny to manage.

We bought our tickets and were faced with a long descent down shallow steps lit by a row of unshaded electric bulbs. At the bottom there was a flat-bottomed boat floating on a narrow waterway tunnelled through the hill when the site had been a working mine.

The boatman was intrigued to find that we were all one party and obviously thought we were quite mad to come on such an expedition with three children under three and three more besides but he made no objection and helped us all to sit down with the more mobile youngsters in the middle. He punted us along for a considerable distance until we came to an enormous cavern in the middle of the hill and we disembarked onto a wooden platform leading on to the floor of the cave. The water poured over the edge into a jet-black lake far below. The noise of the water made conversation difficult but we were able to hear our guide refer to this black hole as 'the bo'omless pit'. Not strictly accurate but the term passed into family usage and thereafter Richard's capacity for food was frequently referred to as the 'bottomless pit'.

On another occasion we set out for Ryber Castle at Matlock, home to a collection of live British wild animals. I parked the car in front of the inhabited part of the Victorian folly, a massive 'ruined' castle on the top of a hill, and reached down for my handbag.

Not there. Panic, as I not only could not pay for our entry tickets but also we were very short of petrol and could not get back to Sheffield without a fill-up. Neither Mrs Faxon nor Nanny Mitch had any money with them either. We sat in the mild drizzle wondering what to do as the children became restless and wanted to get out and see the animals. After a few frustrating minutes a lady came out of the house and approached us. She was obviously wondering why we were still sitting inside the landrover. I pushed open the window and she said, 'Why, it's Dr Wilson isn't it? I used to be a patient of yours before we moved out here. I don't expect you to remember me but you gave me some good advice for which I have always been grateful.'

I explained our predicament and asked if she could not only trust me to send her a cheque for the entry fee but also lend me £2 to enable us to buy petrol to get us home.

'Of course, that's no problem. I'm just glad that I can be of help.'

We soon sorted out the arrangements, the drizzle stopped and we spent a happy afternoon looking at foxes and badgers and comparing the wildcat with the ones we had seen at our remote holiday cottage in the West Highlands.

We spent our summer holidays in Galloway until the increasing size of our family outgrew the available accommodation. Then, in 1960, at the suggestion of Graham's brother, Cedric, we bought a plot of land from the Forestry Commission in Morvern and put up a wooden chalet. That story will have to wait; it merits a chapter, even a book of its own. Suffice to say the third generation are now enjoying the delights of remoteness and the absence of electricity in spite of the unpredictable weather and the summer-long midges.

Four years earlier yet another inauspicious and unintended conception threatened our vacation. We left for Gatehouse of Fleet with the three children, Margaret aged four, John, two, and baby Penelope, only ten weeks old. We always made an early start driving from Sheffield through Barnsley with its miasma of coal and carbolic from the nearby Izal factory, until we reached the A1 near Ferry Bridge. The dual carriage way carried us to Scotch Corner where we stopped at a roadside café to enjoy hot drinks from the outside vending machine. Hot chocolate was the preferred choice but there was one occasion when accidental pressure on the wrong button resulted in oxtail soup being sandwiched between two layers of chocolate without the recipient being aware of it. Graham's reaction when the mixture hit his taste buds has never been forgotten. He never chose chocolate again.

I took the opportunity to go to the loo and was a little disturbed to find I was bleeding slightly. I said nothing at that stage but when we arrived at Miss Carter's boarding house in Gatehouse I was glad to find we were the only guests. Next morning I was bleeding heavily and had cramps in my tummy. I could not possibly go down to meals. Graham coped with me and the children and the anxieties of our landlady. Fortunately we had a good supply of bathing towels and babies nappies of the Turkish towelling variety. They were certainly needed. I lost a great deal of blood over the next few hours but just as I was beginning to think I would have to go to hospital, it began to lessen. We knew that if I went to a gynaecology ward in Dumfries, thirty miles away, I would be kept in for several days, as the custom then was, after the inevitable D&C. Our entire holiday would be ruined but if we managed to cope with the situation, at least the children could enjoy themselves.

On the second day the bleeding had all but stopped and I had no pains so I decided to get out of bed. As I stood up, I fainted for the first time in my life, fortunately falling onto the bed. Graham drove into Kirkcudbright to buy some iron pills and I started taking three a day. It was no use taking more as the body can only manufacture red blood cells at a certain rate, however much iron is taken. I knew my haemoglobin could only rise by 1% a day and it had obviously dropped rather drastically over the past 48 hours.

This was the only holiday when I was delighted to see the rain, day after day. All I needed to do was to sit in the car nursing the baby when we went to explore an ancient monument. I do not think there was one within thirty miles that we did not visit. The Mote of Ur, Orchardton Round Tower, Cardoness Castle, Dundrennan Abbey, Threave (beware the bull), and the graves of the Martyrs at Wigton – the list is endless. We did not cover them all on that particular holiday but how glad I was that the beach was out of the question because of the weather. I could not possibly have walked the few hundred yards to Mossyard Bay from where we had to park the car. I was doubly thankful as my mother came to join us in the second week and I did not want her to find out that I had become pregnant, yet again. Little did either of us know that three more summers were to be affected by unpropitious pregnancies. I do not think she guessed but there were several occasions when my enfeebled state, especially my shortness of breath, would have made the situation very obvious to her nurse trained eye.

I was thirty-two in the autumn of 1959 and had had seven children and a miscarriage in eight years. My three youngest children were all under two and the baby had been conceived when I was wearing a diaphragm and my husband a condom on one of the infrequent occasions when we dared to make love. There was only one possible solution unless we were to remain celibate for the next twenty years; I had to be sterilised.

This was not easy to arrange. Many gynaecologists believed that sterilisation was a form of mutilation and that it was immoral as it contravened the Christian ethic. The Roman Catholic Church still holds this view. I knew all the Sheffield consultants in Obstetrics and Gynaecology in those days and several were personal friends. None were sympathetic to the operation, as I knew from my work in general practice and family planning. It would only embarrass Scott Russell, the professor of gynaecology who lived across the road, if I asked him to sterilize me and it would be the same with any of his colleagues. Fortunately my cousin, Pat Oldham, was a practising GP in the Wirral and she knew a more liberally-minded specialist who might be prepared to help. I went to see him in his rather dingy 'rooms' in Birkenhead, my face powdered white and my slight limp, the only remaining sign of my frequent pregnancies, exaggerated a little. He had no difficulty concluding that another pregnancy would be a serious risk to my health and not long afterwards I was admitted to a two-bed sideward in Birkenhead General and duly had my tubes tied. They were not only tied but a section was taken out from each and I never conceived again.

Naturally my almost constant state of expectancy did not go unnoticed by friends, colleagues and patients. I was working as an assistant with a single-handed lady doctor in Sheffield's northwest suburbs. She was an excellent general practitioner with high standards who kept up-to-date and never spared herself. She had a strong non-conformist ethic and believed that some physical discomfort was good for the soul. Her iron-grey hair was short and straight and the rooms in her house, not only in the waiting and consulting rooms which were part of it, had linoleum on the floor. The only concession was a small skinny mat at the side of the examination couch for those who might be required to have bare feet.

I worked for her three mornings a week from ten until two,

doing 'visits' or house calls, as we would say now. I usually had a
list of about ten or twelve and would then return to base to report.

Mrs Tyndall was in her late seventies. I enjoyed her pithy
Yorkshire humour and lack of self-pity in spite of her almost constant
chest trouble. She also had a very large goitre, a typical 'Derbyshire
neck' which probably pressed on her trachea and did not help her
'tubes' to clear.

Towards the end of my fifth or sixth pregnancy when I opened
the door into the cramped little upstairs bedroom of her cottage
and stood, carrying all before me, she said, 'Ee, luv, tha husband
must be right voracious.'

Poor Graham, a less voracious man it would be hard to find. It
amazed me how well he adapted to the ever-increasing number of
our children. He had been born in 1917 to parents who were already
in their mid-thirties and he remained an only child until he was
nine when his only sibling was unwelcomely conceived, when their
mother was 43. She was a frustrated and ambitious woman who
had kept her husband-to-be waiting for at least eight years before
marrying him, largely, I suspect, because she knew she would have
to give up teaching when she did. She was the head of a primary
school by the time she was twenty-three and really loved her
profession. That she was good at it she demonstrated forty years
later when she taught her first grandchild, our daughter Margaret,
to read, before she started school. Maud was forced to become a
'university wife', become a member of the Ladies Tea Club and
join other 'ladies' in decorating hats or china plates for which she
had no aptitude. She only regained her true role when the war
came and she had to choose between letting Bella, the maid, go to
make munitions or returning to work herself as a teacher. She was
already nearly 60 but she spent five more years doing the job she
was most good at and was a happier more contented woman as a
result. This did not mean that she stopped being an embarrassing
social climber and one who saw social slights where nothing but
kindness was intended.

She was uncomfortable with the social graces and was one of those women who require a month's notice before one arrives for a cup of coffee. 'Dropping-in' was a social solecism to her and Graham had never been able to invite a school friend round for tea without it becoming a major event. Consequently he rarely did so. He once told me that he had promised himself that if he ever had a home of his own it would be open house for all and I think we fulfilled that pledge.

His professional façade as a distinguished medical academic; his reserve and occasional lack of social confidence hid a family man, devoted to his children and tolerant of the many others that were gathered unto us, especially on holidays in Scotland. He was strict over things that mattered.

Unpunctuality and laziness irritated him greatly and child guests soon learnt that absenting oneself when the washing up had to be done was a cardinal sin. A fellow professor once visited us at our West Highland hideaway and told me many years later how amazed he was when he got out of his car after eight miles of extremely rough track, to be greeted by what he thought were scores of children. The great grandmother of all wych elms stood beside the house, festooned with ropes and rope ladders which hung like creepers below the canopy. As the car stopped, the children dropped from the tree shouting a welcome and rushed off to find an adult. There were probably only six or eight actually in the tree but there would have been over a dozen on the site. Graham greeted him, relaxed and smiling and the youngsters duly returned to their ploys. The McGirrs stayed for a meal with us and much regretted that they could not stay overnight (or so they said), as they had to be in Oban that evening. Edward McGirr said it was a revelation to see an entirely different side of this colleague whom he had thought, until then, to be reserved, serious and humourless.

Graham's father was very different from his wife and his continued and genuine devotion to her made me realise that she must have had many redeeming features in her earlier life which were smothered by thwarted ambition and bitterness in older age when I knew her. Malcolm was so much the absent-minded professor in behaviour and appearance that his failure to get a chair only served to rub salt in his wife's wound. He was a distinguished botanist, a specialist in plant diseases, especially those caused by rust fungi but he remained a reader at the University of Edinburgh until he finally retired. He himself seemed oblivious to this academic stop on his career and appeared to be content to pursue his botanical studies and teaching without worrying about his status.

He did not learn to drive until he was 40 and it never became second nature to him. It was quite hazardous to accompany him in a car, as he would forget that he was supposed to be driving. Not long after I became engaged, Graham took me to Edinburgh to meet his parents and in the course of my visit Malcolm came to be driving me up The Mound, the steep cobblestoned road that connects Princes Street to the High Street. I had not passed my driving test (I had not even sat it) or I might have realised sooner that we were losing momentum, and then we ground to a halt.

'Oh dear,' said my prospective father-in-law, 'I'm afraid I forgot to change down.'

On another occasion I was with him on a 'botanising' expedition in the country. We were driving along a relatively narrow road when he suddenly drove diagonally across to a high bank on the other side and came to an abrupt halt.

'I'm so sorry my dear, but there is an excellent specimen of xxx (and he rattled off a long botanical name in Latin) up there.' Whereupon he got out of the car, scrambled up the muddy bank and carefully picked several rather miserable looking leaves from a low-growing plant. He got back into the driver's seat in triumph.

'There you are my dear, a first rate example of infection with yyy. You can see the rusty red sporangia on the underside of the leaf.'

During this interlude the car remained with its bonnet almost embedded into the bank and the body projecting at an angle on the wrong side of the road. Mac had forgotten he was driving a motor vehicle.

He was famously absent-minded. Graham and I arranged to pick him up in Chambers Street after a meeting of the Senatus Academicus of Edinburgh University of which Malcolm was a proud member. We were lucky to find even a temporary place to park and, as we had anticipated, he was nowhere to be seen. While my husband sat impatiently at the wheel in case we had to move off in a hurry, I got out of the car and scanned the pavements. After about five minutes of increasing tension a rapidly moving white balloon on the other side of the street caught my attention. The cars parked in the middle prevented me from seeing it properly until it drew level and then I realised it was Malcolm, the hood of his academic gown, a London DSc, streaming out behind him in the usual Edinburgh wind. He was very apologetic for his tardiness and quite unaware that he had not removed his hood when he disrobed.

Most of his lapses were of no significance but he famously forgot about the farewell dinner in his honour laid on by the Department of Botany at the University. This was a very special white tie and tails occasion and Maud had bought a long evening gown as she and Malcolm were the guests of honour. He went off in mid-afternoon to examine a house said to be suffering from dry rot. He had become an expert, not only in fungal infections, but also in wood worm and death-watch beetle and he was able to earn a little to supplement his meagre university pension by consultancy work in this field.

'Malcolm, don't forget you must be back here by 6.30 at the latest. You've got to change and we are being picked up to go to YOUR dinner at 7.15. Perhaps I'd better know where you are going.'

'No need for that my dear, I don't know myself. This man is collecting me in his car – in fact that must be him now. Don't worry, I'll be back by five at the latest.' And off he went and was not seen again until eight o'clock!

Maud's wrath mounted as the time ticked by and she waited in the hall and then on the steps outside enveloped in her glad rags including the obligatory elbow length evening gloves. The friend who was giving them a lift to the dinner arrived and there was still no sign of the guest of honour. By this time Maud's anger was replaced by anxiety. Something had happened to him, even HE could not forget the importance of the occasion. But he had; he arrived at last oblivious of the storm that was to greet him. He had met a friend when he was on his way home and had gone back to his house with him before making his way back to Kinnear Road. The Guests of Honour eventually arrived at the dinner after the fish course.

Although Maud felt she could never live down the shame (and she certainly did not let her husband forget about it for years afterwards) many of Malcolm's friends and colleagues thought it was an entirely appropriate finale to his academic life – absent-minded, yes, but never about his work, apologetic for the trouble he had caused but freely forgiven because he was much loved and warmly regarded.

Practical Beginnings

In the early days after the war it was not difficult to find part time work in general practice especially if one was prepared to do locum work at short notice. Those were the days of lock-up surgeries in inner cities and standards were sometimes appallingly bad. I remember one surgery, officially timed from 7 to 8.pm. I was seeing my 57th patient as it neared 9oclock when the caretaker appeared rattling his keys.

'That's the last and about time too.'

'Has the other doctor gone?'

'Of course, he's not called One-a -minute O'Connor for nothing!'

During this time I was an active member of the Assistants and Young Practitioners sub-committee of the British Medical Association. In due course I became its chairperson. In this capacity I attended monthly meetings of the General Medical Services Committee. I was given a warm welcome by the only two other women on the seventy-strong body. They all took themselves very seriously and documents involving possible negotiations with the government were marked SECRET and discussed behind locked doors.

In 1954 the matter of the Obstetric List was **the** controversial topic. Feelings ran very high concerning interference with the independence of medical practitioners' rights to practice. In reality this was one of the early measures introduced to protect the public. As the law stood any qualified doctor could deliver a woman in childbirth whether he was experienced or not. It was proposed that an Obstetric List be established within the National Health Service so that only doctors on the list would be paid for the delivery. To be on the list a practitioner had to have had further training in obstetrics, that is, to have gained at least the Diploma of the Royal College of Obstetrics and Gynaecology, or be able to show that he had delivered a certain number of babies per annum over the past five years.

A meeting of all the GPs in Sheffield was called to defend the status quo. Several hundred turned up, more than on any previous occasion. Dr Rushbrooke took me along and, together with Dr Aggie Nutt, we were the sole representatives of the female sex. One after the other the self-righteous males rose to their feet and pompously and angrily defended their rights. Eventually I stood up.

'As the only person here who has ever been at the other end of this situation, I would like to say that I would hate to be delivered by someone, like myself., whose only experience of midwifery is what they have received as a medical student.' This brought the points from the floor to an abrupt conclusion but I do not think my contribution did much to alter the majority view. As with most confrontations between the government and the profession the Minister of Health had his way and the new regulations duly came into effect.

When we returned in the autumn of 1953 from a year in America where Graham had been an Eli Lilly research fellow at Harvard, we knew that Professor Edward Wayne had accepted the Regius Chair of Medicine in Glasgow. This would leave vacant the Chair of Pharmacology and Therapeutics in Sheffield. Graham was the obvious candidate and he was appointed in 1954. Our two and a half bed-roomed pebble-dashed semi was already too small for our increasing family and we moved to a large Victorian house and garden in the old residential district of Nether Edge. At the time we were awestruck by our temerity; but it was one of the best choices we ever made. The house was truly a 'box of delights' for our children; there was a billiard room with a small stage at the back, a coach house with loft over, old stabling, cellars with several rooms leading into a reinforced air-raid shelter with a secret exit into the garden and attics with vertical trapdoors into the roof spaces begging to be made into dens. We spent thirteen happy years there and created a bedrock of positive memories which our children have never forgotten.

After several years as the part time assistant to the spartan Dr Rushbrooke, I left, as she wanted a partner who would be able to make a bigger contribution to her expanding practice than I had time to give. I joined a single-handed Jewish doctor from whom I learnt a great deal about Judaism in our extended coffee breaks. I liked him greatly but thought he was lazy as he left much of the house visiting to me. When he died suddenly of a coronary, aged 44, I was saddened as I looked on him as a friend as well as an employer and my guilt at my superficial judgement of his angina-induced lethargy, remains with me still.

1954 was also significant for me professionally although I did not realise at the time that my professional introduction to family planning would shape my eventual career. The local branch of the Family Planning Association was run by a group of highly committed Non-Conformist and Quaker ladies, who, against the political correctness of the time, were prepared to champion the cause of birth control, especially for the overburdened mothers of the poor. Three women doctors were employed, largely to fit diaphragms, but, sadly, one of them was dying of breast cancer. I was asked if I would undertake a session on Wednesday evenings at the Sheffield Women's Welfare Clinic in Attercliffe for the princely sum of two guineas a week. Attercliffe, in the east end of the city, was only a name on the front of a tram along with 'Vulcan Road' and 'Weedon Street' but I got to know it well over the next decade. After a short apprenticeship I was 'inspected' by Dr Alison Giles who came up from Croydon to assess my competence and I was duly granted my 'Family Planning Certificate' on the 9th of February 1954. Before long I was doing two weekly sessions and the organisation had established several other clinics throughout the city including one in St Mary's Church, which proved very popular.

For the next seven years all we had to offer were rubber goods and two or three spermicidal agents presented in a variety of ingenious forms; creams, gels, foams, pessaries and the strangely popular foaming tablets. Solemn groups of women doctors spent anxious hours discussing whether a cavity rim cervical cap was preferable to a large vimule for a long pointed cervix or whether a watch spring pessary was better than a coil spring. One reason for these deliberations was that in spite of the care and attention given to fitting the right cap into the right patient there was still an appreciable failure rate.

As the years passed I was made personally aware of this in a very obvious way as I conceived and carried to term three children in under two years, the last with my husband using a condom and I a Dutch cap. Masters and Johnson's *Human Sexual Response* published in 1966 made these failures understandable. They demonstrated that during intercourse the vagina balloons to twice its normal capacity and the cervix is drawn up. The hard thrust of the erect penis repeatedly aimed at the target means there is little chance of a neat little rubber diaphragm remaining over the cervix like an Easter bonnet tied below the chin with a bow. The only surprising thing is that most of the time (but not in mine), it did. The availability of an efficient oral contraceptive was an historical event equivalent to the discovery of the circulation of the blood.

Over the course of decades it became known as **the pill** and, in spite of alarms and dire prophecies, especially in the gutter press and the religious weeklies, it has proved to be the biggest factor for change in the lives of women all over the world, than any other single development. It is reliable, safe (less dangerous than an unplanned pregnancy), easy to take, no messing about at the time and no last minute action required before yielding to the throes of passion or even the routine Saturday night dutiful quickie. Now is not the time to enlarge on the history of oral contraception in the last forty years. Many books have been written and there are bound to be many more, but I can testify that it was an exciting time to be in the forefront of such a revolutionary change and to be involved in some of the clinical and scientific studies that have influenced its development. To its everlasting credit, the Family Planning Association took up the new challenge with enthusiasm and laid down medical and administrative guidelines which stood the test of time.

It took several years before the liberating effecs of the pill were translated into action as far as the attitudes of its potential users were concerned. Developments in the means by which it could be accessed were slow and it was well over a decade before free contraception and the involvement of general practitioners were enshrined in law.

Women became aware of the miracle contraceptive but found it was difficult, sometimes impossible, to obtain. It had to be prescribed by a doctor but general practitioners were not interested, they knew little about it and, if they did prescribe, charged a fee. Most local authority clinics were slow to include family planning among the services they offered and many of the Maternity and Child Welfare doctors they employed were only reluctantly involved in contraception. They were more interested in women having babies than in preventing them.

The FPA had an extensive network of clinics throughout the country that charged only a modest fee and the cost of the contraceptives. Many sessions were held in the evening. This suited married working women and the better organised mothers but barriers remained. Family planning was still considered to be slightly improper in the early sixties and women were often too embarrassed to attend locally. For Catholic women this was a particular difficulty and the unmarried also had their problems.

It was against this background that changes in the delivery of services came about within the voluntary sector which antedated the major revolution within the NHS. Clinics like Brook and the 408 Centre in Sheffield, were established to make contraceptive services available to the young, especially the unmarried, and Domiciliary Services were started in many cities for the socially deprived.

In 1974 the government decided to make contraception free to all and to pay general practitioners to provide a service. It was not surprising that a financial incentive would change their attitude from patronising disinterest to demand for over-subscribed training courses. These had to include practical sessions. Many of the older candidates had not passed a speculum since they were students. Sometimes it was difficult to decide who was the most embarrassed, the trainer, the trainee or the patient, but over the course of the next few years almost all those GPs who wished to become competent gained the necessary certificate.

The Den of Iniquity

The Family Planning Association (FPA), like many other voluntary organisations, was managed by a paid secretariat but its policies were decided by a vote of the regional delegates at the Annual General Meeting. I don't know if I was alone in finding the designation of one of these regions peculiarly appropriate – 'Herts and Beds'. The doctors and nurses, who by this time were paid, were also represented. In 1964 the AGM passed a resolution that only those women who were married or about to be married should be allowed to attend FPA clinics. This was an unhelpful victory for the bigot brigade and caused a lot of heart-searching among many dedicated members.

The Sheffield branch had always allowed common sense and compassion to govern their practices and, in effect, no-one was turned away who needed help. The new ruling left us with the unpleasant dilemma of either refusing to see those who were unmarried or suggesting to them that they were going to get married within the next three months. Those who would not connive at this hypocrisy were officially turned away, although a blind eye was frequently turned. Four years later the ruling was reversed and any person working for the FPA who could not agree to a completely open-door policy was asked to leave, and some did. The belief that contraceptive help for those who were not married not only condoned promiscuity but also encouraged it, was strongly felt by a few diehards who, happily, were outvoted in 1968.

As a consequence of this national decision in 1964, Mrs Helen Brook started a clinic in London specifically for the young unmarried which immediately demonstrated the need for its services. In due course others were set up in Birmingham, Cambridge, Bristol, and Liverpool. Meanwhile a small group of doctors in Sheffield led by Jill Tattersall and me, felt strongly that we needed to do something locally. We did approach Brook who encouraged us to the extent of wishing us well and offering £100 as a starter; in return we would be part of their organisation and would be guided by their regulations. We decided we would be better off on our own. We faced a formidable task.

Money had to be raised for what was not only an unpopular but also an unrespectable cause. We wrote begging letters to our better-off friends (not always well received), held wine and cheese parties and dug into our own pockets. An interest-free loan of £1500 from Lawrence Tattersall in addition to what we had raised already, enabled us to buy a small terraced house on a main road not far from the city centre. The first floor and attics were converted into a flat which we had no difficulty in letting to three nurses. This provided a small income and a caretaker. The ground floor was turned into a waiting/reception room with consulting room behind and the 'outshot' kitchen became the nurses' area.

Our fund-raising activities had already engendered a fair amount of publicity and several months before we were able to open the 408 Clinic (it was situated at 408 Ecclesall Road, a major artery from the west into the city centre) women who were no loner able to attend the FPA clinics in the city, began to ask me for contraceptive help. One of my sons was at boarding school and I used his attic bedroom as a temporary consulting room, spreading a folded sheet on the bed and using his Woolworth's angle-poise lamp for any vaginal examination that was necessary. This piece of equipment eventually made its way to the 408 and he never got it back. Thirty years later he still reminds me of this betrayal, especially when he knows he has 'borrowed' something without my consent.

In September 1966 we opened our clinic with some unexpected but very welcome publicity. Splashed across the front of the *Sheffield Telegraph* was the headline 'Bishop Condemns Sex Clinic'. We were interviewed on the radio and before long both the BBC and ITV had short pieces on their screens. There was a wonderful interview with one of our older unmarried clients who was expecting her sixth child in the near future.

'And are you telling me that if this clinic had been here last year you wouldn't be as you are now?'

'That's right, I'm coming right back after I've had this one.'

Fortunately she was not asked why she was there at all, the reason being that she thought she might have caught a 'dose' from one of her clients, advanced pregnancy being no bar to her following her profession in the usual manner.

We also received a lot of unsolicited mail, largely of the vituperative sort. The most memorable was in purple ink on green paper and was addressed to 'The Den of Iniquity' Ecclesall Road. The postman had had no difficulty in deciding that we were the intended recipients. Fortunately several of our clients worked in the media and consequently we had a relatively friendly press but the journalists had no control over the sub-editors who composed the headlines at the top of the columns. The phrase 'sex doctor' contained just the right number of letters to fill the available space. Jill Tattersall, my medical colleague, was involved in a very nasty road accident in that first year. This was duly reported as 'Sex Doctor Injured'. Protests were inappropriate and it served to give the Centre a little more free publicity.

We had no shortage of clients, young women, usually with their

boyfriends (as we called them in the 1960s) travelled from all over
the north and middle of England, from Grimsby to Liverpool and
Matlock to Middlesborough, but over 60% were locals. 457 clients
attended in the first year and 420 of them were not married to
their current partner. At one time I thought I would present this
material as part of an MD thesis but although I collated and analysed
the data, I never managed to finish it. Reading it today, forty years
later, is a salutary experience and brings home the immense changes
in attitudes and practices that have affected social and sexual
behaviour.

Half of the young women were engaged and a further quarter
regarded themselves as 'going steady'. Most of the remainder were
in relationships where one or other partner was married, separated
or divorced. Many were students and few came from either wealthy
or deprived backgrounds. An important part of the ethos of the
408 involved getting to know the client and establishing some sort
of a rapport with her (only three unaccompanied men sought our
help). It soon became obvious that many of them were stressed,
not only by their need for contraception but also by the circumstances of their lives and their relationships. Twenty-two of the
women thought they might be pregnant and fourteen of them were.
One of these was fifteen-year old Sandra, a pretty girl with shoulder-
length dark hair. She was making a great effort to maintain her
composure but as soon as she sat down the words and the tears
could be held back no longer.

'I don't know what to do, I'm sure I'm pregnant.' Her middle
class voice, with a trace of the local Yorkshire accent only served to
emphasise her distress.

'I'm always regular and my period is three weeks late now and
I was sick before breakfast this morning.'

'So, how did it happen?' I asked gently.

'Mum and Dad have gone to the Bahamas for six weeks and
left me with my sister, Sonia. The weekend after they left we had a
party and I'm afraid I had too much to drink. I'm not used to it,

you see. I don't really remember what happened but I woke up about five the next morning and found myself on the floor behind the settee with my pants off.'

'What did your sister do?'

'Oh, I couldn't tell her, in fact I haven't told anybody – I'm not even sure who the boy was. . .' she tailed off miserably.

'Well, first things first. It may just be anxiety which is delaying your period,' but alas, it was not as a pregnancy test on her urine demonstrated.

I attempted to examine her vaginally but her hymen was intact.

'You don't use tampax then?'

'No, I tried once but I couldn't get it in so I always use pads.'

She had conceived without penetration which was really the most appalling bad luck, but not without precedent.

In late December 1966, nearly a year before the passing of the Abortion Act there was nothing that could be done and the consequences for herself, her baby and her family were potentially catastrophic. She was under the age of sixteen and sexual intercourse with a minor even without full penetration, was and is, a felony, a criminal offence. Her parents were due back the next day but I thought it unlikely that they would report the matter to the police as not only was there no evidence to implicate a particular man (this was decades before DNA testing) but they themselves were not without guilt. To go abroad for six weeks and leave a fifteen year old in the care of her eighteen year old sister was not very responsible.

'I'm going away with friends on a skiing holiday in the Alps the day after tomorrow. I'll have the holiday first and tell my parents when I get back.'

Even as she spoke, she smiled in anticipation of the fun she was going to have and reminded me of the child she still was. She was a brave lassie but she lived more than fifty miles away and I never learnt what happened to her.

Cathie was forty-two but looked older. She was neat but shabby and sat on the edge of her chair mangling a sodden handkerchief in her restless hands. Twenty years before she had had a boyfriend with whom she had 'walked out' for nearly seven years but both had observed the conventions and chaste kisses were as far as it went. Eventually she had realised that his relationship with his widowed mother meant more than his love for her.

'I can't leave her at her age,' he explained, but when she became aware that his mother was fifty-six and worked full time as a 'buffer girl' in Mappin and Webb's, cutlery manufacturers, she broke off the friendship. She had not found another partner until she was approaching forty. He was a Catholic and she was C of E and her elderly mother and her twin sister strongly disapproved. She hoped to persuade them to give her engagement their blessing when tragedy overtook them. Her sister was found to have advanced cancer of the breast and Christine moved in to look after her, her husband and three children. Her sister died but she stayed on. The bereaved husband and his family depended on her. There was much less support for single parents of either sex in 1966 than there is now. Occasionally she managed to meet her fiancé but she had no access to contraception and now she feared she had 'fallen'.

'I'm that desperate, doctor. There is no way I can have this baby. My nerves are shot to pieces. I'd rather take my own life than let my brother-in-law suspect the truth and I know it would kill my mother.'

I suspected that her mother was as tough as old boots but it was no use saying so and Cathie's distress did amount to an acute anxiety state. She was neither sleeping nor eating and could concentrate on nothing except her predicament.

There was a remarkable woman gynaecologist in Newcastle at that time – Miss Kerslake. I knew that in some circumstances she would terminate a pregnancy if there were medical grounds. We knew the law was going to change shortly but far too late for Cathie. I thought it was worth referring her especially if she had a strong endorsement for the procedure from a consultant psychiatrist.

There would be no problem about this. Dr Lawton Tong was a founder member of our 408 committee, a pillar of strength with a fund of common sense and a great sense of humour. He guided our tentative venture and we met him regularly to discuss both general and specifically patient-related problems of a psychiatric or psychological nature. I managed to speak to Miss Kerslake on the phone and put the case to her as succinctly as I was able. She was a formidable lady and not given to inessential conversation.

'Phone my secretary and tell her I've agreed to see this patient on Thursday next.' That was it. In due course Cathie returned for contraception, after a short stay in Newcastle.

It was my first hand experience with the women attending the 408 that convinced me of the need for legal abortion. Thirty-one women had had a previous pregnancy and thirteen babies had been adopted. Their young mothers were middle or lower middle class, six being students. They contrasted with the eighteen who kept their infants, more than half of whom were working class and living on National Assistance. Two were students whose parents were caring for their children while the daughters studied. One of our clients was a prostitute who was expecting her sixth child but she 'signed on' after the birth.

Interviewing the girls whose babies had been adopted was a harrowing experience. They were still grief-stricken and guilt-ridden years after the event. They would know exactly how old the child was and cried bitterly as they described how they were pressurised into giving up their infants. In those days 'disgrace' and 'letting the family down' were over-riding considerations, frequently even greater than the financial ones. Years later when abortion had become an accepted part of the contraceptive scene I rarely encountered similar grief in connection with an unwanted pregnancy. Most women accepted termination of the pregnancy as an unpleasant but necessary expedient and several told me with no expressions of regret that this was not the first time they had resorted to abortion. Indeed in Russia and Eastern Europe abortion has been the principle method of birth control and thousands of women have had more than ten.

Evelyn was one of my most memorable patients. She was a plain rather angular woman whose slightly bulging short-sighted eyes were not concealed by spectacles. She was in her early forties and wore a neat brown felt hat to match her coat and skirt. She looked what she was – the 'treasure' of the office in a highly reputable solicitors.

She sat down composedly and smiled revealing an attractive and intriguing personality.

'I need a reliable form of contraception for three months.'

'You seem very sure of the time you will need it,' I smiled back.

'The father of my son is returning to Argentina before the end of May and I won't need anything after that.'

'Your son?'

'Yes, I left him with the nurse outside – I thought you would need to examine me and it seemed easier to leave him asleep in his pram.'

My thoughts were turning somersaults, I had imagined a teenager and now here was a baby!

'He is six weeks old and I had my postnatal check yesterday. Everything is all right and the scar has healed nicely so I thought it was only fair to Jaime to resume our relationship for the few weeks that are left before he goes home.' More somersaulting, this was not a legal separation or divorce.

'Perhaps you had better start at the beginning and tell me about it,' I suggested.

'Well, I'm forty-four, and have a good job in a solicitors' office – I'm the senior partner's personal secretary. I lived with my mother in a comfortable house in Nether Edge (an older residential suburb in those days). I had had one or two male friends but nothing serious and I'd become very set in my ways, not perhaps MY ways but my mother's ways. I wasn't unhappy but it was so dull. Then my mother died suddenly of a stroke and I realised what a lonely and unfulfilled future I had to look forward to. I decided that if I had children my whole life would be transformed.' She paused.

'So, did you find out too late that the man was married?' I asked.

She looked at me in astonishment.

'Oh no, I wanted a man who was already married. I had no intention of spending the rest of my life with a man. Marriage was not an option I seriously considered. What I wanted was a child, children in fact – but that is no longer possible,' she added sadly.

She told me she joined the Spanish Institute, which not only ran language classes but also had an active social side where people who were Spanish speakers could meet fellow Spaniards or South Americans and mix with English people of similar interests in their language and culture. She had deliberately cultivated a friendship with an Argentinian doctor who held a research fellowship at the university for a period of eighteen months. She knew he was married and had three children in South America. She was quite open about what she wanted and promised him that she would make no claims on him if a child were born. They must have had a great deal of trust in one another and she was also blessed with unusual luck. She conceived within three months and had no problems in the early months of her pregnancy. She confided in her employer who agreed she could take maternity leave and return to the office part-time when the baby was six months old – a very unusual and tolerant man he must have been.

Then her luck ran out and she developed acute thyrotoxicosis six weeks before the baby was due. Her overactive thyroid gland made her very ill and permanently affected her eyes so that they would always be a little protuberant, not due to short sight as I had wrongly concluded. She was admitted to hospital but her heart was seriously affected and the infant had to be delivered by Caesarian section three weeks early. Even so he was healthy and thriving although she could not feed him herself as she had intended. She was stabilised and her cardiac problem had been sorted out but she had been told that a further pregnancy would jeopardise not only her health but her life.

'I can't possibly risk anything happening to me, I'm all that William has. . . it's a shame because I planned to have TWO children to keep each other company, especially as I get older. There would just have been time to conceive again before Jaime has to go back, I had it all planned. Anyway, that's why I need contraception, you see.'

Over the next few months before I left Sheffield, I saw her several times in the local shops with young William in his Silver Cross pram proudly parked outside by the windows. One cannot help speculating on what he is doing now, over thirty years later. I hope he is not still living with HIS mother.

The staff worked for nothing in that first year but by 1969 the 408 was self-financing. Before long the doctors, nurses and administrative staff were paid the same rates as their equivalents in FPA clinics. The Centre continued to provide a specially youth-oriented contraceptive and sexual health service within the NHS for the young people of Sheffield until 1999 when it was shut down by the Sheffield Community Health Trust.

The Successor to
the Hound of the Baskervilles

In 1959 Dr Mary Peberdy introduced the first home visiting service into family planning practice. She was a real pioneer and worked in Newcastle where there was no shortage of suitable clients. She had a considerable degree of success, which was all the more remarkable because this was in the late fifties before the pill. Caps and condoms were the only methods available and I came to learn from my experiences later that these methods are not popular with those who live in poverty. The lack of privacy and running hot water and the distaste for 'messing about down there' made it very difficult to use a diaphragm effectively.

I came to know Mary through an entirely different aspect of her work. The RAF became concerned about the rising number of pregnancies in the Women's Auxiliary Air Force. Such unfortunate accidents were nothing new to the women's services. When my husband was first commissioned into the RAF as a very green young medical officer, he was posted to a fighter station where there were a number of WAAFs. Towards the end of his second week he was holding a sick parade which included a young woman.

'Well, what's the matter with you?' he asked her.

'Nothing really, it's just that I think I've got caught.' Even my husband, wet behind the ears as he was, knew what she meant. After dealing with the medical side his thoughts turned to the future welfare of mother and child. 'You know you should be able to claim some maintenance from the father?' She looked doubtful. 'He ought to give you something towards its support.'

'It's not that easy.'

'Why not? If he is a serviceman he can easily be traced.'

'No, no, it's not that. It's like this Doctor, if you cut your finger on a circular saw you wouldn't know which tooth it was that dunnit.'

The RAF in 1962 recruited a panel of seventy professional women, mostly with family planning or marriage guidance experience to provide courses in 'Personal Relationships'. We each received a letter from the Air Ministry covered in 'secret' and 'confidential' labels inviting us to attend the Ministry in London but with no indication of what we were wanted for. The top brass found the whole matter intensely embarrassing. We almost had to sign the Official Secrets Act before we were allowed inside the building. We discovered immediately that those medical officers who were to guide the 'officers and gentlewomen' (ie, the commissioned recruits) were more senior, experienced and better connected were taken off to a place apart and we never saw them again.

Mary and I were among those allocated to the raw recruits who had their basic training at a large RAF station near Grantham. We had to go in pairs about every two months. Each new intake was given a day in which to grasp the fact that if you have intercourse a pregnancy is likely to result but that you can take precautions to prevent it. We had to play down this essential bit of information because the WAAF was, publicly at least, very conscious of the need to maintain moral values, ie, say 'no'.

The Commander of the station was Dame Jean Conan Doyle, the daughter of the creator of Sherlock Holmes. We were taken to meet her in her office and she was friendly enough but showed little of the imagination for which her father was famous. Her main interest, on that day at least, was her whippet, a pet of extraordinary unattractiveness whose enormous eyes seemed on the point of dropping out of its skull. It lay curled up in a dog basket at her feet. I don't think the impression of devotion to her canine companion was entirely misplaced as, at a later date, we found the whole camp in disarray as all personnel, officers and recruits alike had been detailed to hunt for the animal which had absconded. Obviously Conan Doyle's investigative genes had not been passed on to his daughter. The animal must have been found as by lunchtime everything was back to its usual torpid rhythm.

The only way Mary could reach Grantham from Newcastle by 9.30am was to travel by rail to Sheffield the night before. Then we made a very early start, usually by car but sometimes by train, depending on the weather. At first we were worried in case we might arrive late – there was a lot of fog between Sheffield and Grantham in the winter in those days – but we soon realised that our fears were unfounded. The working day of the officers was from ten to twelve thirty and then from two to four. Our 9.30 arrival was timed to allow us a cup of coffee with the staff and to start the day in a civilised fashion. Lunch was in the officers' mess preceded by a drink at the bar, which we prudishly usually refused. The Medical Officer was a colourful character who told us he had had 'a bloody good war'.

'I managed to get some bloody good shooting wherever I was stationed – the duck shooting was bloody good in Egypt. . . ' He was a man of very limited vocabulary. 'See this tankard? See that bloody great dent in it? Well that happened in Burma. I was stuck in that bloody hole, Imphal, surrounded by the bloody Japs along with a lot of other fellows. We used the radio to our chaps and they would drop the supplies we needed. Well, I thought if we are going to be stuck here for a bit I must have my own tankard, I'd had it with me ever since the war began. Even though it might be bad luck if I didn't have it with me.

'Damn it, I'd survived so far, hadn't I, and I'd been in some tight corners before. So, I asked them to drop it to me with the rations and the ammo and they bloody well did. I was a bit upset when it hit a rock on landing but now I'm bloody glad it happened. It's an honourable battle scar, what? Gives me a bloody good chance to shoot my mouth off, like I'm doing now.'

The niceties of service protocol were a source of constant amusement to us. Indeed I think lay women often find many of the traditions and practices of men in formal organisations, whether it be in the RAF, the Courts of Law or the Houses of Parliament more than a little ridiculous but we know we are more likely to reform them by a 'softly, softly' approach. Certainly Mary and I never made any open comments but we did catch each other's eye when observing a more than usually lunatic bit of nonsense. (And I believe the RAF is nothing like so steeped in these observances as the Army). We enjoyed our days at Grantham with the raw recruits, some of whom were not yet kitted out in their uniforms. Most had left school with few certificates of any kind and yet they had the courage to strike out on their own and join the WAAF

Mary came to stay for a weekend before we started. We made a list of topics we felt must be covered.

'We've got to give them some idea of the menstrual cycle and conception before we can even start on **contraception**.'

'Surely they must get that at school?'

'Some may but I bet most of them get no farther than the birds and the bees.' So it proved. We would start by explaining about periods with plenty of time for questions. Most girls are not embarrassed by talking about 'the curse' or 'my monthlies' or (in Scotland) 'ma illness' as long as the company is all female. Period pains, tampax, being caught unawares loosened their minds and their tongues. We did not ask whether any of them used tampons or whether they had tried and had problems.

'It's a good idea to have a go with the tampon when you haven't got a period. Lubricate it with a little Vaseline and then squat or put one foot on a chair. Most people think their front passage – that's called the vagina – goes straight up inside like going up to the north pole and coming out at your tonsils but it's not like that at all. You can see from this that it actually goes backwards. . . '

We produced the pelvic model which the FPA used for demonstrating the fitting of a Dutch cap. The model was far from aesthetically beautiful, being made of hard pink plastic but it did give a three dimensional view of the relationship of the pelvic organs which was much more realistic than the usual diagram of a pear sitting in an elongated egg cup with two extended and droopy branches each ending in a little round walnut.

It was easy to go on to 'What if it's late?' This was a lead into conception about which there was almost universal ignorance.

'When is the safest time in the month if you don't want to get pregnant?'

We were aware that this was hardly the P.C way to pose the question but communication was the name of the game.

'Please, Doctor, it's okay in the middle isn't it?' was a fairly standard answer.

We would draw a diagram on the blackboard, a horizontal line divided into four sections.

'Each section is one week, seven days. Most girls' periods last around five days, give or take two days either way.' We had to be careful not to arouse anxieties if one of our audience did not conform to the average. The first five sevenths along the line were crosshatched accordingly.

'Now all through these days the egg has been ripening in the ovary and in the middle of the month, day fourteen if you are regular, it pops out of the ovary into the open end of the tube. . . '

We went on to contraception, spending most time on the pill and encouraging questions but the majority were reluctant to speak up in front of their peers. We told the girls we were going to talk about V.D. and then personal relationships in the afternoon. We said we would leave a box with a slot in the lid for people to leave anonymous questions which we would try to answer before the end of the day.

The part the recruits enjoyed most (according to their evaluation forms) was when we divided them into groups and gave each set a question to discuss which involved 'personal relationships'. This was *Woman's Own* stuff.

'I love my boyfriend but he says I don't really because I won't go all the way.'

'My period is late and I don't know what to do.'

There were problems about organising group work because the course was held in the base cinema. The seats were not banked but were fixed in rigid rows and it meant that at least some of each group had to twist themselves round or sit uncomfortably perched on the back of the seat in front, but they did not seem to mind.

The questions in the box covered a wide spectrum and displayed a depth of ignorance which the morning's talks had obviously not succeeded in plumbing for everyone.

'My boyfriend holds me very tight when we are dancing. Can I get pregnant that way?' (These were the days of tangos and quicksteps).

'Is it bad for you to wash your hair when you have a period?'

Sometimes a more serious problem was revealed.

'Every time my boyfriend wants to make love to me I throw up as soon as he touches me. I mean I'm sick all over him but I know I love him. Is there something wrong with me?'

This last was very difficult to answer. No good saying 'Go to the doctor'. We could imagine the crude ridicule with which the 'bloody good' medical officer would greet such a problem. The reply had to be given in public and generalised. This girl needed skilled counselling and the only place she had of finding it was in certain Family Planning clinics, which ran psychosexual counselling sessions, and there was certainly not one in Grantham. We suggested that anyone who was worried because they could not respond properly to their boyfriend's lovemaking (this was years before 'partner' became the correct term) should wait until they were home on leave and then phone the nearest clinic to find out where they might find advice. This was the best we could do. I have often wondered since whether she received the help she so obviously needed or whether she ended up without a close relationship with anyone of either sex. Perhaps she became a career woman and the WAAF equivalent of a company sergeant major. She almost certainly had been sexually abused earlier in her life but in the sixties this was a taboo topic even with most of the medical profession.

Mary and I became good friends over the three years we worked together in Grantham. Early in 1967 I was staying with her overnight after contributing to a Family Planning training course in Newcastle. The phone rang while we were having dinner. 'It's for you.' I was surprised. Graham and I had never been ones to ring one another when we were away from home unless it was important. This time it was.

Mary and Geoffrey must have seen something in my face.

'Well?'

'Graham has just been confirmed as the Regius Professor of Medicine in Glasgow.'

Whenever Mary enquired after my husband in the future she always referred to him as 'Old Reeg'.

Below the Waist and Above the Knee

My husband was invited to become the Regius Professor of Medicine at the University of Glasgow in 1967. He was fifty and well aware that if he did not make a move he would probably remain in Sheffield as the Professor of Pharmacology and Therapeutics for the rest of his working life. He had held this position for fourteen years and rightly believed that it was time both he and the department had a change. I was not so keen but, of course, there was no real choice.

'I'll go,' I said, 'but I won't pretend I want to.'

I worked in general practice for three sessions a week. Officially these were of four hours but in reality I rarely got home before three, having started at half past nine. For this I was paid £600 p.a. without pension or insurance contributions. I also did three venereal disease clinics a week. The 408 Centre for the young unmarrieds was in its first year and I was much involved; I had started a small home visiting project providing a contraceptive service for what were known in those days before political correctness inhibited our language, as 'problem families'. I was effectively running the medical side of the Sheffield family planning service and I was a member of the Clinic Doctors National Council of the FPA, which met monthly in London.

In view of these commitments it was not surprising that I was reluctant to uproot myself and move north. I was faced with decisions about my professional future. I had to make a choice between general practice and family planning and the wider aspects of reproductive health, especially of women. I loved being a family doctor but I knew I must either be fully committed to it and drop my other interests or remain an underpaid and undervalued part time assistant. I was already heavily involved in the FPA's training programmes and in other specialised areas of clinical work in the field. I knew that the move to Glasgow would present challenges which I believed I was well-qualified to take up. The invitation to do three weekly sessions in venereology tipped the scales and, once in Scotland, I was no longer engaged in general practice.

It was difficult to find a house big enough for six children and with an adequate spare room for the numerous visitors we had, not least the external examiners. Graham was determined to be within reasonable walking distance of his department in the Western Infirmary and the schools into which our children had been enrolled. It was then, and still is, an awkward journey from Sheffield to Glasgow and finding a suitable dwelling place was, as it had been in the past, left to me. We were fortunate in having friends who were both willing 'to watch the papers' ie, the weekly property issue of the *Glasgow Herald* and keep their ears to the ground for any possible houses.

'I know we are going to end up with one of those ghastly terrace houses about six floors high with two rooms on each floor,' I expostulated. Indeed, we were offered just such a one by the University in The Square but I rejected the suggestion immediately when I saw inside, behind the imposing façade. I am sure the Department of Law is much happier behind its grey walls than we would have been.

Eventually we did buy a terrace house, on four floors with three main rooms at each level. It was a good choice and one we never regretted although it took the family some time to adjust to not having any real garden except the communal one across the road and surrounded by a fence. The activities that were allowed within the hallowed precincts were governed by rules laid down by the Gardens Committee which was composed of old women of both sexes. Football in particular was virtually proscribed, as were all games in the forenoon on the Sabbath.

As a consequence Richard and the Gibson boys (their father was Alexander Gibson, Musical Director of the Scottish National Orchestra) who lived two doors along, played in the street, there being far fewer parked cars and much less through traffic thirty years ago. It was not long before two residents, a deputation in fact, called on me to remonstrate about their activities. I was not completely surprised as I was far from happy myself about their playing in the road and was concerned not only for their own safety but also for possible risks to property that might result from an ill-judged ball.

The two ladies seated themselves, not altogether comfortably, on my settee. Consequently I was somewhat taken aback by their opening remark.

'We wondered whether it would be possible for the boys to wear their school games clothes when they are playing outside?'

'Well, I suppose it might, but whatever for? Richard is wearing out his old prep school rugby shirt that he used to wear in England and the Gibson boys were sent their green and white ones by a relative.'

'That is jut the difficulty, your son's is **green** as well.'

'I'm sorry, I don't understand.'

'We know that all three boys attend Glasgow Academy which has a navy uniform. Green does lower the tone of the neighbour-hood so and is not really acceptable to most residents in the Gardens.'

This was not quite the first time I had been brought face to face with the bigotry and prejudice of the Protestant element in Glasgow.

I had been approached by the Consultant in Venereology, as the specialty was unambiguously known in 1967, to work for three sessions a week in his department with a view to providing, in addition to the usual clinical services, contraceptive advice and methods for those women attending the V.D. clinic who would benefit from free access to family planning. I would be seeing female patients only as, traditionally in Glasgow, women doctors were only supposed to have tough enough susceptibilities to treat males if they worked full time in the department. I had been seeing men and women with venereal problems for over three years in Sheffield but once across the border my vulnerability altered, unless, of course, I worked full time. The nurses who worked at Black Street, the main venereology clinic in the city, were both health visitors who not only had a small caseload of families for whom they were responsible in the usual way but also did the contact tracing and the clinical work in the women's part of the unit.

They were the salt of the earth and knew more about the regulars, Betty's Bar and the Chinese boats than one would have thought possible for two unmarried, middle-aged and gently reared ladies. However we all have our weak spots. I decided we would have to have separate case sheets for the contraceptive part of our client's care. Once they had completed their treatment and follow-up tests the women would not like to be reminded of them every time they returned for a further three months supply of the pill. It would also be much easier for the doctor if the two matters were kept separate. For some perverse reason female patients had blue case sheets and men pink, while white, surely the colour of innocence, was allotted to the few of either sex who were syphilitic. I was asked to decide on a colour for the family planning patients.

'Green would be rather nice.'

Dead silence, and a mask-like lack of expression on the faces of the two nurses. The senior clerkess stepped back a little.

'I think you had better choose another colour, Doctor. What about yellow?' said Sister Anderson. I had no wish to be difficult and was happy to agree but I had no idea where I had gone wrong. Some time later I asked Margaret, the clerkess, where the problem lay.

'It was because you had suggested **green**, that's the colour of Celtic you see.' By that time I was indeed beginning to see.

In 1964 I had started working in the Department of Venereology at the Royal Hospital, Sheffield. I had had no previous experience in this specialty but at least I was competent with a speculum when examining female patients. The consultant in charge, Robbie Morton, was an enthusiastic and intelligent teacher with a great sense of humour. His short round cheerful presence stimulated the staff not only to work hard for their patients but also to extend the boundaries of their knowledge and play an active part in research. All the medical staff were expected to present a paper to the department at least once every three months. Even I, with only three sessions per week was not excluded from this duty. Once a week the clinic was closed to patients an hour earlier than usual to allow time for a staff meeting at which a presentation would be given, problems discussed and we could be updated about recent advances in the field. The topics chosen were extremely varied and ranged from the results of different treatment regimes to the social backgrounds of different groups of clients. On the wall of the staff room there was a large-scale map of Jamaica into which were inserted between thirty and forty coloured pins.

'What on earth is a map of Jamaica doing on the wall?'

'Have you seen any cases of yaws yet?'

'No, I don't know much about it.' In truth I knew nothing except that it was a disease that occurred in the West Indies and was caused by a spirochaete, like syphilis although it was not sexually transmitted.

'We see quite a few cases here, mostly in men from Jamaica,

They have a positive Wasserman Reaction (the antibody test for syphilis) and so they are often referred here for treatment from some other department. Of course once we have established the true diagnosis we can reassure the poor man that all he has is yaws and not syphilis. We can treat them easily enough as outpatients. We've become mini-experts on yaws. One of our last registrars made a note of the district in Jamaica in which the man had been brought up. It's a disease of poor hygiene and poverty. It causes ulcers on the skin and in bad cases the bones can be affected as well. It happens in childhood when some trivial break in the skin becomes infected from contact with a lesion in another child. You can see that nearly all our cases of yaws, the red pins, come from rural areas outside Kingston while the blue, uninfected men, are concentrated in the capital where there is a reasonable water supply and washing children is much easier.'

Not long after this I saw my first case of yaws, in a pregnant young West Indian woman who had been found to have a positive Wasserman reaction at her antenatal clinic. The clear-cut partially pigmented scars on her shins were characteristic and she said she had had them since childhood. She did not have the much less common 'sabre tibia' which indicates a severe infection and involvement of the skeleton. There is one beneficial side effect of this unpleasant but rarely fatal disease in that the infection appears to confer a relative immunity to syphilis whose causative agent, *treponema pallidum*, is closely related to it. We gave the young woman the usual course of penicillin just in case there was any lingering infection, and the reassurance that, as far as yaws was concerned her baby would be fine and healthy.

The Glasgow department was very different. There was strict segregation of male and female patients geographically and administratively. The staff were separate except for the few full time doctors who did clinics in both areas. We only saw our colleagues on 'the other side' if we had lunch at a nearby canteen. Even those who worked on the same side had little contact with doctors who did different sessions and there was no communal medical staff room or weekly meeting. This was much less mentally stimulating than the Sheffield department but nevertheless I spent twelve happy years at Black Street and was spared the ultimate move to modern custom-designed accommodation within Glasgow Royal Infirmary with no windows or access to natural light, by resigning when I became full time Clinical Coordinator of the Glasgow Family Planning Service.

Glasgow did have its compensations. The female clinic at Black Street was small and did not have many staff. There was a communal staff room where we gathered for coffee mid-morning and the atmosphere was friendly and relaxed. Margaret the receptionist and Betty the secretary tried to finish the crossword in the *Glasgow Herald* before I managed *The Times*. They were usually successful and I was not. During my time there we were rarely what I would call busy by the standards of other types of clinic elsewhere. Patients had open access and did not need an appointment for a first visit so we never knew how many to expect apart from those tracked down by the contact tracers and those returning for further treatment or tests of cure. I usually took some other work with me, such as writing up domiciliary family planning case notes if I had time to spare. I know that once the move to the Royal Infirmary took place, things changed but I am glad I was part of that friendly caring unit when time was not rationed and we were able to give each individual more than just a genital examination and a dose of pills. I am sure efficiency does not preclude these extras but it does tend to put them on the danger list.

Lizzie was a semi-permanent inhabitant of Woodielee, a large mental hospital on the outskirts of the city. She was brought to Black Street as it was thought, correctly, that she had gonorrhoea. A male patient had complained of a discharge, quickly followed by five more from the same ward block. It did not take long to find out that Lizzie had been running a nice little business in the huge linen cupboard where the folded sheets provided a ready-made couch comfortable for one, or more, persons to lie on. She gave her favours in exchange for cigarettes and would probably not have been found out if she had confined her clients to those within the hospital. Unfortunately for her, she became greedy, or perhaps she just wanted a change. She had inveigled a punter from the big wide world outside who had introduced the gonococcus into the sheltered life of the mental hospital. She was a simple soul in terms of IQ as she had been born with congenital syphilis, contracted from her mother while she was still in the uterus, and this had affected many systems in her body. She had been diagnosed at birth and treated accordingly so that the spirochaetes had been eliminated for good but the damage they had done could not be repaired. In spite of this she was quite capable of managing her affairs to her own advantage, as she had clearly demonstrated. She was short and slight and her face had the appearance of an adult baby but, at 32, it was easy to see why she had no difficulty in attracting clients, although I thought her looks would have been improved if she had kept her teeth.

While I examined her and took the necessary swabs, I talked to her conversationally to keep her mind off what was happening down below.

'What happened to your teeth Lizzie? Did they all go bad at once?'

'Naw, it wiznae like that Doctor. They wiz verra guid teeth but some o' them wiz a funny shape. Every time I went to see a doctor aboot anything, sair throat, pains in ma belly or whitever, they took nae notice as soon as they saw ma teeth. They'd get a' excited an' ca' in their pals tae look at ma mooth an I couldnae get onymair sense oot o' them. So, Ah jist decided Ah would have then a' oot and Ah've had proper medical attention eversyne.'

What a sensible if drastic solution I thought. The teeth of congenital syphilitics show characteristic deformities; the front ones are notched – Hutchinson's incisors – and those further back have only one cusp instead of four and are known as Moon's molars. I had only seen one patient with this condition before and that had been as a medical student in the forties. Even then all pregnant women had a blood test for syphilis as soon as they presented for antenatal care. It never occurred to anyone to ask their permission, it was 'just routine'. A positive test was rare but after the war there were women who had become infected by their men and knew nothing about it until the result of the blood test meant they had to suffer a long course of penicillin injections, which would cure them and their unborn babies. Although the spirochaete would be killed if they had the full course of treatment, the antibodies in their blood would remain, a permanent marker of the original infection.

One afternoon the waiting room was unusually full. We rarely had more than two or three patients waiting, but on this occasion there were eight. Two were old hands returning for their final check-up but the others were all new. There is rarely much conversation between clients in a V.D. clinic, which was just as well in this instance. I called out the number of the next new patient. Anonymity was vital in the waiting room, but once in the consulting room a friendlier atmosphere prevailed and I invited the attractive twenty-year-old brunette to take a seat.

'What's brought you here?' I enquired.

'Well, my boyfriend told me I should come for a check-up as he's had a bit of trouble. He say's he's caught something from his previous partner, though he split up with her months ago. He says it sometimes takes a long time to come out?'

'Yes, well, it's very sensible of you to come. We'll soon know if anything's the matter. Most infections clear up pretty quickly if you have the right treatment. Have you had any other partners recently?'

'Oh no, James is the first man I've ever been serious about. We're going to get engaged next month but I want to be sure everything is alright first.'

Poor wee lassie, she certainly had a 'dose' (gonorrhoea) as I could see when I examined the swab down the microscope. Fortunately the treatment is straightforward and short but she would have to return at least three times for routine tests of cure.

The next patient was a good-looking but more mature lady in her late thirties. She was in a state of acute anxiety as she had been having an affair until her lover advised her to 'go for a check-up'. She was terrified her husband would find out and had already aroused his suspicions by her inadequate excuses for avoiding intercourse.

'It's always sex on Saturday and golf on Sunday and he knows my periods are as regular as clockwork.'

She also required treatment and would have to find an excuse for several weeks more.

The next girl, hardly more than a child, was fair and pretty but could hardly stop crying, her handkerchief a useless ball in her fingers.

'I don't know what to think, I'm sure he wouldn't be unfaithful, we love one another but he said I'd better come because he thought he might have caught something from a lavatory seat. I went to a bookshop and pretended to be looking for something on the pill but I looked up V.D. in a health book and it said you can't get it from lavatory seats, it has to be from another person.'

She also was infected as were the three other victims in the waiting room. James was certainly a very active and obviously attractive man who had managed to convince at least six women that each was the only love of his life! We already knew of his activities as he had presented himself to the male clinic and, on being found to be infected had been asked for a list of all his contacts. He had been told to tell each one that she needed a check-up and warned that if they did not turn up a contact tracer would go and visit them. It was not unusual for a man to list several conquests, indeed many were proud to do so, but James was unusual in naming six who all attended on the same afternoon and none of them ever discovered, as far as we knew, that the others existed.

Jeannie was an old customer. She and her sister treated Black Street like an annexe to Betty's Bar, their regular pick-up point along the Broomielaw by the Clyde. In the late sixties there was still a remnant of activity in what remained of the docks and the prostitutes made the most of what there was.

'Well, Jeannie, what's the story?'

'Ah wiz working the Chinese boats, ken, so Ah need a check'

'Okay, how many sailors did you go with?'

'Och, Ah couldnae tell ye that. Ah lost count. Ye jist get passed roond, know what Ah mean. Any road, Ah was pissed oot o' ma mind maist o' the time.'

'When was that?. Which night would it have been?'

'It was three-four days last week. Ah cannae mind exactly. Ma man wiz awfy worrit.'

'I'm not surprised. I'm sure you were too drunk to let him know where you were.'

'Naw, naw, it wasnae that. He kent fine where Ah was. He sent me. Naw, ken, Ah cannae swim.'

She then explained that access to the 'Chinese boats' was by a narrow gangplank with no handrails. Last week there had been two boats moored alongside one another and the only way the crew of the second boat could reach the shore was by means of a plank bridging the gap between them. Negotiating this in the dark when far from sober would indeed be a hazard.

Two weeks later her sister did fall into the dock and was rescued with sufficient drama to merit a minor headline in the local press. No doubt the heroic policeman did save her life because she 'couldnae swim' either. No mention was made as to what she might have been doing on the dockside at two in the morning.

Tragedy sometimes walked through our doors. It was a warm stuffy afternoon and we had had only one patient since lunch. I heard the receptionist booking somebody in, slid *The Times* crossword out of sight and straightened myself in my chair. The door opened and Margaret ushered in an elderly woman who looked as though she would have bolted had she not been kindly supported to a chair beside my desk. It took a long time to sort out her story but fortunately there was no hurry. Miss McLeod had been engaged to a soldier in the Argyll and Sutherland Highlanders in the early years of the war. She had been brought up in the 'Wee Free' Kirk and it was only when her fiancé was to be posted overseas that she eventually succumbed to his entreaties and they had sexual intercourse the night before his departure. Her remorse and guilt are difficult for today's generation to understand but they were to dominate her life and eventually cause her death. Soon after the event she noticed a slight vaginal discharge and immediately attributed this to venereal disease, which she interpreted as the wages of sin. She was far too ashamed to seek medical advice and, indeed the symptom soon went away. The physical reminder of her sin had gone, but fear and guilt remained. For weeks afterwards she was certain she was pregnant but that also proved to be unfounded. She continued to write to her Jim but never mentioned her anxieties or feelings of shame. Six months later he was killed in the Western Desert.

She went to the library to look up 'venereal diseases'. She did not understand most of it, (medical dictionaries in the public domain were far from user-friendly in 1943) but concluded she had syphilis and that was why her symptom had disappeared. She was certain the germs remained in her and that she was therefore potentially infectious to anyone who came in touch with her. This belief prevented her from ever allowing herself to become close to anyone of the opposite sex; she denied herself the possibility of marriage and children. Almost worse, she would not allow members of her own family or their children, whom she loved dearly, to embrace her and would not even stay in their homes overnight in case she contaminated their bathrooms with her deadly germs.

She believed God was punishing her, but eventually the development of increasingly distressing symptoms had forced her to seek medical advice. As she attributed them to venereal disease she had come to Black Street, and, as she said, 'I couldn't possibly go to my nice GP and tell him I had blood coming out from down below.'

I had been aware from the moment she sat down that she was suffering from something far more deadly than burnt-out syphilis. The insidious cloying stench of rotting tissue surrounded her and I knew what I should find when we finally persuaded her that she had to be examined 'down below'. Maureen, the state-enrolled nurse, stood beside her at the head of the examination couch gently persuading her to talk about her much loved nephews and nieces to take her mind off what I was having to do at the other end. The smell was dreadful but one learns to be a mouth breather if one works in a genito-urinary clinic. I cleaned the vulva of blood and discharge and gently slid a small speculum into the vagina, mopping out the disgusting debris to reveal at the top, a whitish yellow mass, like a rotting cauliflower, which replaced all the normal tissue. She had an advanced carcinoma of the cervix of the uterus. I referred her to an understanding gynaecologist at the Royal Infirmary as an emergency but, as I feared, the disease was too far advanced to treat and she died three weeks later.

She had first noticed traces of blood nine months before and had she sought help then, it might have been curable. Ironically, it was probably that one act of sexual intercourse which would cause her death forty years later. We know now there is a close association between a particular strain of the genital wart virus and subsequent cancer of the cervix. This virus is almost certainly sexually transmitted. Although it was a first and once for her, it was certainly not the first for him.

A very different client was a remarkably self-assured young woman who presented a contact card at reception. Her boyfriend was, I discovered, a macho youth with a motorbike and she rather fancied herself as his 'moll'. She was newly fifteen, well-spoken and should have been at school, studying. Unhappily she did have gonorrhoea and so had to return several times. I raised the matter of contraception with her. She was basically a sensible girl and was pleased to have advice and, more practically, be given free supplies of the pill to start on the fifth day of her next period. I duly filled in a yellow card but at her second visit suggested that rather than returning to the V.D. clinic for her contraceptive supplies, she might prefer to see me in Claremont Terrace, the main family planning centre. She thought this was a good idea and we arranged a suitable appointment three months ahead.

About a week later there was an insistent banging on the door of the clinic which was locked during the lunch hour. Margaret opened it to be pushed aside by a furious man insisting on seeing the doctor in charge. In due course he was persuaded to calm down enough to explain his wrath. He had found our anonymous appointment card in his daughter's blazer pocket and phoned the number, ostensibly to change the time but in reality to find out what it was for. He demanded to know why he had not been informed that his daughter attended, what was the matter with her and whether she had had any treatment. The premises at Black Street were not large and he was making such a noise that it was natural for me to join the group at reception.

I told him immediately that I had been the doctor who had seen his daughter and invited him into the consulting room to discuss the matter. He continued to expostulate but was persuaded to sit down. I let him carry on until he ran out of steam and I studied him as he did so – late forties, around five foot eight, smartly turned out in a military style raincoat, his brown leather shoes highly polished. He had a small black moustache and short back and sides and looked exactly what he was, an ex-major in comfortable civilian employment whose whole world had been turned upside down by discovering that his much loved fifteen year old daughter was attending a V.D. clinic.

It was a long time before he would accept that I could not tell him what as the matter with his child until I had her permission. When he saw that I was adamant he admitted that he knew already that she had been infected and treated. When he had challenged her with the appointment card, they had had a tremendous row and she had hurled the truth back at him in a desperate attempt to cause the most pain.

'You see she is so different from her two older sisters. They did so well at Hutchie's (Hutchison's High School, a much-respected grant-aided secondary school in Glasgow), passed their exams and went on to university. Fiona seems not to care. She started going out with this appalling lout with the motorbike she met at some disco. He's totally unsuitable, hasn't got a brain in his head and how he can afford a bike heaven only knows because he doesn't appear to have a job. We stopped her seeing him, we thought, but it made no difference. Then we said she had to be home by nine o'clock. When that didn't work we locked her into her room for the weekend.' He paused.

'Well,' I responded quietly, 'I don't expect that worked either, did it? It would just make her even more determined to disobey you.'

'No, it didn't. She got out of the window and climbed down the drainpipe. Of course, I knew where she would go. We have a holiday house in Inveraray and she has friends there. I know the local police sergeant and asked him if he would meet the bus from Glasgow and keep her until I arrived by car to collect her.'

I thought this small victory for the forces of right and order had done little to help the situation. I tried to help him to understand that Fiona (she was more often referred to as 'my daughter') was rebelling against authority, particularly HIS authority which may have been a little less relaxed than that in some of her friends' families; this did not mean she did not love her parents but that the way forward lay in talking to each other. I encouraged him to decide that out-and-out interdicts would only drive her farther away and that next time she might go for good, even to

London, where the chances of finding her before she was seriously damaged were slim indeed.

'If you can just let her get herself through this phase without too heavy a hand, she is sensible enough, underneath the rebellion, to want more for herself than a pillion seat on the back of a 350cc motorbike. If you threaten her with 'never darken our doors again' she might take you at your word. Relax the rules to more realistic parameters – midnight instead of nine o'clock, no embargo on the boyfriend etc. Get your wife to agree and all three of you discuss it sensibly together.'

He looked up, embarrassed. 'Well, the truth is, my wife doesn't know anything about all this.'

Therein, perhaps lay the root of Fiona's unhappiness and her drive to rebel. What sort of a relationship was there between a husband and wife when they could not confer in such a desperate situation? No doubt much of the ex-major's anger lay with himself but I do not think he had much insight at that moment. He nearly exploded once again when I said, 'And what about the pill?'

At length he agreed that contraception was better than an unwanted baby and he left more quietly than he arrived.

Fiona continued to attend Claremont Terrace but about a year later she said she would not be coming back as she did not need the pill anymore. She had given up her boyfriend as she was concentrating on studying for her Highers as she wanted to go to university.

A consultant vacancy occurred in venereology in 1979 and I was asked to apply for it. It was a full-time appointment and carried the appropriate salary. I think the head of the Sexually Transmitted Diseases Department (as we had been re-christened) thought I was mad to turn it down. I had no higher qualifications and nowadays such an appointment would be impossible but in those days experience and the strong recommendation of the 'chief' would certainly have secured it for me. The choice was similar to that in 1967 when I had had to decide between general practice and family planning for the main thrust of my professional life. Now the choice lay between a reasonably well-paid virtually 9-5 job with no weekend work, in a specialty in which I had worked for sixteen years. In spite of this experience I did not really believe I was an expert. There were areas of venereology in which I had little expertise, especially with syphilis and non-specific urethritis. Indeed I had not seen a male patient with a sexually transmitted disease since I left Sheffield in 1967. These deficiencies could have been made good by appropriate extra training.

No, the fundamental reason was that again I felt committed to family planning and all the wider aspects of women's health that this embraced. I knew I WAS a specialist in this field and my involvement in the clinical, administrative and training arms of this increasingly important branch of medicine was total. Never mind that the pay was peanuts and the hours as long as I chose to work them, that was where my heart lay and I had no qualms about turning the offer down. It was a decision I never regretted.

Inside the Uterus

In 1963 we were hearing of another method of contraception, not really new but the modern development of an older device. The Graffenburg ring had been made of gold or silver wire tightly wound into a flexible watch spring which could be inserted through the cervix into the cavity of the uterus. It was said to be used by wealthy young socialites before they made the nineteen twenties equivalent of the 'grand tour'. It had been effective but had fallen into disrepute when it became associated with infection and even malignant disease. The idea of an intra-uterine device had been taken up by Lippe who used a form of flexible plastic which could be straightened out for a short time so that it could be passed through the narrow cervical canal and then resume its original zigzag shape once released inside. We family planning doctors in Sheffield were very keen to include this method in our contraceptive armamentarium but there were difficulties. Only Dr Margaret Jackson in Exeter was fitting these devices outside London. She had never discontinued using Graffenberg rings in suitable recipients and, as she checked her patients regularly, her patients had no trouble.

The new plastic devices were an easier and much cheaper development, which she welcomed but her support was of little use to us in Yorkshire. They were also being used in a clinic in Westminster Hospital and in the North Kensington Women's Welfare Clinic, run by the FPA. We received permission to go there and observe the procedure.

Dr Margaret Curtis and I travelled to London on the *Master Cutler*, a wonderfully dignified, comfortable and noisy steam train that reached the capital by 10a.m. The premises at North Kensington, dingy and dark green did not impress us and the staff did little to dispel the rather depressing atmosphere. The first patient was waiting on a hard chair in a corridor outside the small room in which the procedure was to be carried out. She had apparently been told as much as it was felt she needed to know on a previous visit. A grim-faced nurse in late middle age opened the door.

'Komm,' she said in a strong mittel-european accent. The woman climbed onto the couch and lay on her back with her knees bent and her feet on the bed, wide apart. A green surgical drape was placed over her lower body. The doctor stood at the end of the couch, poised ready for action.

'I'm just going to examine you first.' No reply was expected or volunteered.

The speculum was inserted; a pair of forceps was attached to the cervix to hold it steady and a thin blunt probe or sound, was passed to measure the length of the uterine cavity. This obviously caused some discomfort and the patient caught her breath.

'Won't be long now, it doesn't really hurt,' said the doctor. She picked up the slender plastic introducer tube and threaded in the flexible Lippe's Loop with its two trailing nylon threads and then pushed the solid rod down the tube until it met the end of the loop. 'Mustn't be too long over this because the plastic only has a ninety second memory and it won't regain its shape after that.'

She steadied the cervix with the forceps and pushed the loaded introducer into the cervical canal. The woman cried out but gritted her teeth as the device was extruded into the uterus. The threads were cut to an appropriate length, the instruments removed and the woman told to sit up.

'Come along. No need to make zuch a fuzz,' said our 1960s nightingale. The patient was taken out and seated on the same hard chair on which she had been sitting ten minutes before. I never heard her name. She was still sitting there holding her tummy and looking rather faint when it was time for us to go.

There were two more patients that morning neither of whom seemed to experience the same degree of pain and discomfort that had been felt by the first. We were allowed to pass the sound in both these ladies but were firmly told that we would have to attend six sessions as **observers** before we would be allowed to actually insert an IUD. After that it would depend on our progress. We thanked our mentors and escaped out of that rather negative establishment. We had learnt a great deal more than we realised, mainly about how **not** to run an IUD clinic, but our immediate reaction was dismay. There was no way we could afford the time or the money to undergo this training in London. That seemed to be that but fate was kind.

Leafing through an old FPA Newsletter I noticed a small advertisement.

'Doctor on leave willing to train f.p. doctors in IUD techniques. Reply to Dr Betty Knowles.'

Some time had elapsed since the ad had been inserted so we did not manage to contact her until she had already reached the UK. She was spending the Easter term in England while she settled her two sons into a prep boarding school in Yorkshire before returning to her family planning post in Fiji. We had ten weeks. She was a Sheffield graduate who had worked in maternity and child welfare clinics for the city in the past. We arranged for her to do a locum for a colleague on maternity leave in the same department and one of our lay committee members had a furnished flat available to rent. Dr Knowles was able to live nearby and train as many of us as we were able to organise. We had to find the patients first; at least five for each of four sessions per week. It was a sign of the huge hunger for freedom from unwanted pregnancy that we had no difficulty in recruiting as many as we needed and the demand for the method continued for years afterwards. It was popular because once inserted it required no further action on the part of the user after the first six week check had been made.

The only device we had then was the Lippe's Loop, in batches of ten in a little plastic bag, which were shaken out into hibitane solution and then loaded into the introducer with dissecting forceps. We had no disposable plastic gloves and had to use rubber surgical gloves, boiled and put on while still wet. Betty Knowles trained five of us in those crowded weeks and we subsequently instructed scores of family planning doctors from the middle and North of England. Inevitably we had a little difficulty in persuading the powers that be that we were as skilled as our southern colleagues and that our 'graduates' were as well taught as those in London. As we had far more experience and had many more IUD insertions than any other FPA clinic, our expertise was acknowledged in the end. Presenting authority with a *fait accompli* and demonstrating that it is successful is a technique I found useful in other situations.

Glasgow had come late to intra-uterine contraception. The Scots tend to have a greater reverence for those in authority than I was accustomed to. If a consultant, or, even more, a professor, made a statement it was rarely queried. As I was married to one I had an inbuilt advantage as I had certainly not promised to obey, but even without the benefit of my conjugal experience, I think I would still have been less accepting than my colleagues.

Ian Donald was the Professor of Obstetrics and Gynaecology in 1967. He was a great man, an engineer before he turned to medicine and had invented the ultra-sound machine whereby soft tissues could be pictured within the body. On our arrival in Glasgow he invited me round his department and demonstrated the machine on a pregnant woman. It was a very special moment for me and one I one I have never forgotten. I had heard of ultra-sound but few hospitals were using it routinely at that time.

In spite of his eminence and kindness I was aware that I knew more about IUDs than he did but it was going to be a little tricky to change things without upsetting a great many people. Women who wanted a 'loop' as it was called then, (later this changed to 'coil' as better devices came along) were advised and examined at the famiily planning clinic and were then referred to the gynaecology out-patient department at the Western Infirmary on a Friday morning at 9 a.m. They were not allowed to eat or drink after midnight the night before and, on arrival, undressed and put on a short operating gown and long white woolly operation stockings. They then went into an operating theatre and, once on the table, their legs were hoisted up into stirrups. The build-up was enough to frighten all but the most determined. It was no wonder that some patients fainted and most felt unsteady and sick for some time after the insertion. Starvation, nakedness, bright lights and a hospital environment were calculated to produce exactly those reactions. I knew from hundreds of IUD insertions in Sheffield that while there were occasional adverse reactions of which one had to be aware, the great majority of women could have the device fitted with very little difficulty. The more relaxed the patient, the less likely she was to feel faint or experience cramps.

In due course the women of Glasgow were able to enjoy the same arrangements as their Sheffield sisters and have their IUDs fitted at their convenience in a family planning clinic or even in their own homes if they were patients of the Domiciliary Family Planning Service. This had been established in 1970 and from the beginning we realised the advantages of inserting intra-uterine devices in the patient's own home. Many of our clients disliked clinics, especially when they knew there was a good chance they would be asked to take their knickers off and be examined 'down below'. They were poor time keepers. It was no good making a home visit before 10.30 a.m. at the earliest – even then they were unlikely to be dressed. Morning appointments for whatever reason were rarely kept. The Dom service took people as they found them, unwashed, smoking and with the only too obvious olfactory evidence of the binge the night before. These women knew we were there to help them in a very practical way; they did not want another pregnancy at that time and they knew their own unreliability about taking a pill every night. They wanted something they would not have to be responsible for, which they could forget about until they wanted it out. For many, the coil was their choice and we gave it to them.

One of my most memorable experiences with an IUD was when I was doing the procedure in a patient's home. Margaret Wallace 'chapped' the door of the tenement flat, one floor up, on Maryhill Road. Nothing happened and I bent my head to the letterbox and pushed up the flap. The unmistakeable smell of poverty billowed out – urine, unwashed clothes and bodies, stale cigarette smoke.

'This is certainly the right house,' said Sister Wallace (in Glasgow the dwelling house is always 'the house' regardless of its dimensions). In the darkness of the landing it was difficult to be sure of the name but 'One Up Left' was what was written on the notes.

'Try again.'

This time we heard someone fumbling with the catch and the door opened revealing a small slight girl about six years old wearing a very short rather grubby dress and an overlarge cardigan with the sleeves rolled up to her wrists.

'Ma Maw sez youse to come ben the hoose.' She led the way in the semi-darkness into the nearer of the two rooms. Mrs Cunningham was sitting in her inadequate nylon nightdress on the side of the bed that was recessed into the wall. It was not much wider than a single bed but the usual size for a married couple in an old Glasgow tenement. It was not ideal for acting as an examination and operating table, but it was all there was.

'Just lie back across there with your head up in the corner by the pillow and your feet on the bed in the opposite corner.'

She lay back, completely relaxed once she had lit her cigarette, the eight month old baby resting in the crook of her free arm. Meanwhile Sister Wallace had put down her deep wicker shopping basket in which she carried all that we were going to need, including the furled triangular off-cut of purple rubber-backed bathroom carpet. I was very impressed by this piece of equipment as it was not only of great practical use (the floors were always filthy) but it made me realise that some people actually had fitted carpets in their bathrooms. We were still in the lino era at home.

I knelt on a fairly wide base and did the necessary vaginal examination. It was a little tricky as the patient's left foot had a tendency to slip off the bed but I passed the speculum without difficulty. I was inserting the sound when, to my horror, an Alsatian's head emerged from under the bed so that its slavering jaws were centimetres from my nether regions. The canine pants and perhaps an involuntary intake of breath on my part alerted the lady on the bed.

'He'll no hurt ye, Doctor. He's jist being friendly.'

I completed the insertion in record time and carefully moved back. Sure enough he 'didnae hurt me' but his friendly overtures had included a liberal licking of all my adjacent parts he could get his tongue to.

Hundreds of IUDs were inserted in patient's homes by the Domiciliary teams in Glasgow without any adverse reactions or late after effects. I am sure this was due to the relaxed atmosphere and the confidence the women had in the doctors and nurses who visited them.

In 1970 Dr Robert Snowden, at that time a lecturer in the department of Social Studies at Exeter University, set up a research group of twenty family planning clinics to establish unbiased trials of new intra-uterine devices. Glasgow was one of the participating centres and in the spring of each year the same medical coordinators foregathered on one of the widely spaced buildings of the campus for our annual meeting. Bob was the chairman and Liz, his wife, was in charge of administration. We accomplished a great deal especially in the early years before the influence of American overkill made even the enrolling of a patient into a clinical trial so time-consuming that fewer and fewer were prepared to do it.

For several years I stayed overnight with Dr Margaret Jackson who was already past the usual retiring age. I flew from Glasgow to Heathrow late on a Friday afternoon at the end of the day's work and hired a car to drive to Reading. This was in the days before the M4 and finding ones way through Hillington and Uxbridge to reach the A4 and on to Reading was not easy. Leaving the car parked in the station I caught a train to Exeter St Davids and by 9.30 was in a taxi en route to the family planning clinic where Margaret would be closing up as I arrived. Even by the standards of those days it was far from up-to-date. Two large nappy pins held the curtains together across the front of one of the cubicles. A microscope was set up on a bench and was in regular use as she was primarily a medical gynaecologist. She was as interested and knowledgeable about the flora and fauna of the vagina as she was about the plants in her beloved garden at Crediton. She was medically educated in the time before equipment was disposable and used a metal teaspoon rather than a pipette to procure a liquid specimen to place on the glass slide and view down the microscope. No doubt she had more than one and no doubt it was boiled up in the steriliser after use but I remember my astonishment and hope I did not show it.

Margaret was a true pioneer and had established a highly successful artificial insemination service using donor sperm decades before it became part of the NHS infertility services. She had no qualms about the rightness of her actions and had no ethics committee to convince or submit to. The donors were frequently of healthy farming stock and she carefully selected them as she did the aspiring parents. She was a strong believer in the benefits of stable marriage for the future well-being of children. If she thought there would be problems in the relationship, the couple would not be accepted. Robert Snowden followed up the lives of many of these A.I.D. children in 1978. He showed that for the most part Margaret had chosen their parents well and as a result a higher than average number were stable and prospering.

The drive back to Crediton, six miles away, was not without its hazards. Her car was far from new and her ancient and rather smelly canine hearthrug, Mo, had to be persuaded into the back seat, a move that was openly resented. I was aware of the doggy breath growlingly expelled beside my right ear as her head forced its way between me and her mistress. The animal had some reason to be annoyed as the back seat was already crowded with rugs, containers of garden produce and the large wicker shopping basket in which Margaret transported all her medical equipment, occasional case notes, and often half a dozen fresh eggs for a friend. The road between Exeter and Crediton was not very wide and rarely straight. She always drove down the middle and only moved over if she had to, but at least at night one could see the oncoming headlights before the vehicle came round the bend. Once home, the sitting room fire was poked into life and we sat drinking whisky and talking until I was forced to seek my bed. I feel I came close to this very remarkable lady in a way that would not have been possible without the dim fire-light and the toddy. She had had several major tragedies in her life and I had had one or two but our talk ranged over many things and often included laughter, or, more frequently, wry smiles.

A record was kept of every IUD fitted in each of the twenty clinics. The Exeter University unit soon became involved in clinical trials of new devices as well as monitoring those already established. The Dalkon Shield was a popular device with both the family planning doctors and their users. It was not suitable for women who had not had a child, but it was easy and quick to insert in the multiparous. Reports were published regularly and in 1974, 173 pregnancies had occurred in over 4000 users, a comparable figure to the pregnancy rate with other devices.

By this time there was a growing amount of bad publicity for the Shield from the US which asserted that it was associated with pelvic infections and septic abortions. In 1977 the Unit had records of over 40,000 IUD fittings of which 7282 were Dalkon Shields. The pelvic infection rate in these users was on a par with other devices and it had the lowest perforation rate. Two septic abortions were reported; both in Glasgow and known to me personally. One woman was sleeping rough and had contracted gonorrhoea prior to the miscarriage. The other, almost certainly, had tried to induce an abortion illegally with a knitting needle.

These findings did nothing to support the American case but such was the panic and subsequent litigation that A J Robbins, the manufacturers were destroyed. In 1980 the company, supported by the International Planned Parenthood Foundation recommended that all women wearing the devices should have them removed. In the face of such advice it was difficult not to comply but, as I was aware through our membership of the FRRN (Family Planning Research Network), the British figures did not support this view. I compromised by not systematically recalling every Dalkon user but offering her the choice of keeping it *in situ* or having it taken out when she presented for her routine check. Most wanted them out because the UK press had, as always, aped the American scaremongering but a few kept their device and were none the worse for it. Apart from the totally unjustified demise of AH Robbins, there was a global downside as the popularity of intra-uterine devices decreased significantly and has never really recovered.

It was as well that by the beginning of the 1970s the sticky problem of the need to obtain the husband's consent had more or less been resolved. The question had arisen in 1965 before I left Sheffield and inevitably recurred in Glasgow. I wrote to my Defence Union concerned about a worn-out wife who had three small children. She had used a diaphragm successfully following Vatican

II but then came the Papal Encyclical *Humani Vitae* in 1968. Her husband who professed to be a devout Catholic, although he had not been to Mass since the baptism of his youngest child, insisted that it was now 'against his religion' for his wife to use birth control. It was apparently not against his beliefs to demand intercourse as his right five or six times a week regardless of the time in his wife's menstrual cycle. The woman was desperate and fear of pregnancy was causing increasing mental ill-health.

I wrote to the Medical Defence Union and stated that **my** duty was to my patient whose health was being jeopardised and that I was not responsible for her husband's conscience. I asked if he would have grounds for an action against me if I fitted a device against his wishes. If so, was a wife legally bound to bear a child when she did not want one, even if this impaired her health or even endangered her life? The response of the Defence Union was 'we cannot advise that an IUD should be inserted contrary to the husband's direct wishes', although, by 1968 they added that 'where the health of the mother makes further pregnancy a threat she is entitled to ask a doctor to prescribe a method which she handles herself, such as a diaphragm or the pill.' In those days the legal opinion of the medical profession had advanced little beyond the Married Women's Property Act of 1882.

I have no record of when this advice (or the law) was changed but I never asked for the husband's consent either in Sheffield or Glasgow.

Amazingly this archaic attitude continued to be enforced on British women even in 1987 in that last bastion of male prerogative, the Armed Forces of the Crown.

Nancy Loudon was my opposite number in Edinburgh where she ran a first-rate contraceptive service with close ties to the University. High quality research and training were carried out at the headquarters clinic in Dean Terrace. She is typical of the best Scottish women medical graduates, intelligent, hard-working and meticulous. She ran a tight ship and did not suffer fools gladly but her warm friendly personality softened the edges and made her an excellent leader of her team. Characteristically she was married to a consultant gynaecologist, also an Edinburgh graduate, who was held in sufficiently high esteem to be a Vice President of the RCOG (Royal College of Obstetricians and Gynaecologists) in London. Both live out their professional lives in the city where they trained as undergraduates and where they hope to spend the remainder of their days.

Nancy was elected chairman of the National Association of Family Planning Doctors from 1980-1986 and was largely respons- ible, with her husband John working behind the scenes, for the eventual adoption of the Association by the College as the Faculty of Family Planning and Reproductive Health. This translation did not actually happen until three years later, under a different chairman, a man. The wheels of gynaecology grind exceeding slow, the gestation period from the conception of the idea to the birth of the new faculty being more like nine years than nine months but the infant was mature and healthy at the time of its delivery. As a result the RCOG benefited to the tune of £100,00 and family planning finally became respectable at the cost of loss of autonomy and the inevitable pressures of male dominion and power politics.

Nancy had asked me to join her and two senior nurses in putting on a family planning updating course for the SSAFA (Soldiers' Sailors' and Airmen's Families Association) nurses with the British Forces in Germany. These women acted as health visitors to the families of servicemen, usually in the army but there were some RAF stations as well. No base could be left 'unmanned', and as the smaller stations only had two nurses, the SSAFA staff were divided into halves and we did the course twice. We enjoyed the week greatly and were impressed with the calibre of the personnel. We also learnt a lot about the arcane mysteries of service life and the difficulties of being a service wife. The written consent of the husband was required before a woman could have an IUD inserted by the medical services of the crown. Some women were so incensed by this that they travelled back to the UK at their own expense to have their device fitted even when their husband had no objection. This was a costly business for a private's wife and demonstrated their strength of feeling.

The popularity of the IUD as a contraceptive method fell away as the century advanced and by the time I retired it was difficult to find sufficient cases to train the next generation of doctors in the techniques of insertion and removal. This was a pity as it is a method that suited many women who did not want to have to think about 'taking precautions' on a daily basis.

Clinical Culture Shock

On moving north I was aware before I arrived that the practice of family planning in Glasgow would present something of a culture shock. The dignified lady doctor representing that constituency on the Doctors National Council always wore a large wide-brimmed hat, adorned with artificial flowers or fruit or sometimes both, which stayed firmly on her head throughout the proceedings. She was unique in this but was nevertheless respected for her forthright, if conservative views. One of the other senior doctors was retiring from clinical practice and I was asked to fill the vacancy. I had been a Senior Medical Officer, recognised as a Trainer since 1962. We overlapped for a week or two and I was fascinated to observe that on arrival at the clinic she changed her outdoor coat for a white one but left her hat on her head. As it was of the close-fitting toque variety it was less likely than her colleague's to fall onto the patients abdomen when she was performing a vaginal examination and no doubt it was secured by several long hat pins.

Dress was not the only old-fashioned aspect of medical life at 27 Lansdowne Crescent, the headquarters of the Family Planning

Association in Glasgow. The two large front rooms of the residential tenement flat had each been divided by thin wooden partitions into three cubicles. As in many public lavatories, the dividers did not reach the ceiling, while curtains inadequately covered the fronts. In one room the large Victorian fireplace jutted a yard into the room so that the small space was further reduced and it was extremely difficult to stand at the end of the examination couch.

I had been given a warm and friendly welcome and it was not for me to voice my reservations. I was a stranger in a strange land and came from England, however much of a Scot my father's genes made me. I started one Wednesday evening in early October. Many of the patients were young married working women for whom this clinic was the only place they could obtain medically prescribed contraceptive supplies. General practitioners were not interested in family planning in 1967 and had little financial incentive to become so. If her doctor was willing to prescribe, the woman paid him 7/6 or ten shillings (38p or 50p, quite a lot in those days) for a private prescription for six months' supply. She took this to a chemist who kept it and sold her one packet of pills every month for which she paid not only the retail price of the product but also a dispensing fee on each occasion. The practical difficulties of following these procedures were almost impossible for working women but three-monthly, later six-monthly, appointments at an evening FPA clinic made contraception a reality for hundreds of thousands of women. They were also aware that doctors who worked in such places had a genuine interest in, and considerably more knowledge of the subject than the average GP. A careful medical history was taken and the patient's blood pressure was routinely checked at every visit.

I sat behind my desk and the nurse ushered in the first patient.

'Do sit down Mrs MacPherson, how have you been getting on with Conovid E (a contraceptive pill)?'

'I'm fine, they're great and I haven't put on weight as all my friends said I would,' she succinctly replied. She beamed happily while I looked in her notes for a record of her blood pressure. Not seeing it I opened the sphygmomanometer and unwound the cuff while she took her arm out of her sleeve. I wrapped it round her upper arm and listened to the sound of the blood pulsing through her brachial artery as I slowly released the pressure. By the end of the evening I realised that, in Glasgow, the doctor was expected to take every patient's BP whether they were attending for the first time or it was just a routine return visit. As I drank a cup of coffee with my colleagues at the end of the session I asked, 'Do the doctors always take the blood pressures?'

They looked at me in amazement.

'Of course, that's a medical responsibility. And, in any case, the nurses aren't trained to take BPs in Scotland.' It was my turn to be surprised.

It took some months and a great deal of tact and persuasion to encourage the nurses to undertake the task. Most had never been taught how to do it but their willingness to try was greatly helped by the presence of two younger nurses, trained south of the border, who proved to be skilled and competent. Even so, there were two old battleaxes who refused to learn but they were supremely capable of teaching nervous young women how to fit their diaphragms. The nursing duties were allocated accordingly. The remaining difficulties lay with some of the doctors. In spite of being informed that it was the norm in most FPA clinics for nurses to perform this task, certain of the medical staff were very reluctant to let go. No doubt some felt it was an erosion of their expertise and felt threatened by any delegation of their traditional role. Some thought they would be legally liable if a nurse made a mistake and the patient's health suffered as a result. Twenty years later I was horrified to discover that a doctor in a peripheral clinic was still insisting on taking all the blood pressures herself in spite of repeated reassurances that she would not be legally responsible as the nurses had been properly trained and assessed as competent.

I realised then, as now, that those who were most reluctant to change in this and many other aspects of progressive medical practice, were those who were the least secure. Family planning attracted women doctors who wanted to do part time work, usually because they had young children. Most subsequently found careers in other branches of medicine but it was interesting that many of these continued with their once or twice weekly sessions and undertook further training and experience to become senior clinical medical officers in addition to their roles in general practice or hospital medicine. There were other young doctors who believed their duty to their families was overriding and with whom, even after six or seven years of hard grind and a great deal of tax payer's money, medicine came a very poor second. They joined retainer schemes 'to keep their hand in' and had to undertake at least two clinical sessions a month. Family planning was an obvious choice from their point of view but I always felt that doctors with a wider clinical base made better clinical medical officers. Good contraceptive practice involves the health of the whole person and often that of the partner. In the old days of rubber goods and chemicals, general medicine played little part but the licensing of hormonal products and intra-uterine devices demanded both skill and knowledge. I believed lady doctors earning a little 'pin money' were no longer appropriate practitioners.

Sex on the Rates

The poverty, overcrowding and degradation of thousands of families in Glasgow only twenty five years ago are difficult to convey to those who have not seen it. It was obvious to me that family planning could make a real impact in such circumstances. It was no good expecting those who needed it most to attend clinics to seek advice. Following the examples of Mary Peberdy in Newcastle and Dorothy Morgan in Southampton, I started a small one-woman home visiting service in Sheffield, taking the pill to what were known as 'problem families', on a regular basis. I bribed my way in initially by taking children's clothes in the back of our landrover and soon found the women were pathetically grateful to find that they could also have free instant family planning. Sheffield was a prosperous city then with low unemployment and the 'problem families' were only a very small proportion of the population. Glasgow was teeming with rat-infested tenements and vast acres of rundown housing schemes without amenities or civic pride. It was a wonderful place to see if taking contraception to the homes of the people who needed it, really could make a difference.

The medical officer in charge of Family Planning Services at Lansdowne Crescent, Dr Lorna Naismith and I were invited to the City Chambers to meet the Health Committee to discuss our request for a small grant to fund a home visiting service. Labour held an overwhelming majority in Glasgow and its support came from huge working class wards with big Roman Catholic populations. In 1970 one third of the people of Glasgow were Catholic but there was a class bias so that Protestants predominated in the middle class areas and Catholics in the housing schemes. They voted Labour if they voted at all and there was a Catholic majority on the Health Committee. The chairperson, Mrs Nan Patrick, was self-evidently of that persuasion and yet, such was her concern for the poor women of her city, that she was prepared to listen to our proposal. We wanted to start a pilot scheme in a wedge-shaped section north of the River Clyde with the apex at Lansdowne Crescent and the triangle widening out to the city boundary to embrace Maryhill and Springburn. We asked for £2000 to cover the cost of staff, supplies, administration and transport. We had some telling ammunition with which to persuade the committee.

A report published in 1970 entitled *Born to Fail* detailed the progress of a cohort of over 10,000 children born in the United Kingdom in a single week in February 1954 and followed up by the National Children's Bureau. This demonstrated that a child's physical, intellectual and emotional development was closely correlated to his or her social circumstances at birth. Three criteria of disadvantage were identified: low income, poor housing and family size of four or more siblings or the mother being a single parent. Children who suffered from all three – the severely disadvantaged – were more ill, did less well at school and were more likely to be known to the social services. The report found that while one child in twenty was severely disadvantaged in England and Wales, the proportion in Scotland was one in ten and half these children lived in Strathclyde.

The other publication was just as damning. The Scottish Home and Health Department published a report in 1971 on 'Infant Mortality in Scotland'. Among many other facts it analysed death rates by social class and place of domicile. This showed that in Glasgow, 12 out of a thousand legitimate babies born to middle and upper class mothers would die in the first year of life (the number for all classes in the UK is now 7 per thousand) whereas illegitimate babies of mothers of social class V (unemployed or unskilled) had an infant mortality rate of 77 per thousand, almost one in ten, comparable with figures from parts of the third world.

In our presentation to the Health Committee we said, 'As doctors and nurses we can do nothing to improve low incomes and poor housing but we **can** do something about family circumstances. We can help mothers to restrict the number of their children to those they can cope with and provide practical help to young single mothers so that they don't have another baby before they are ready for it.'

'And how are you going to go about it? Knocking on doors and forcing your way in to folk's houses. It's no right,' said one aggressive male committee member.

'No, it wouldn't be like that. The woman would have to be asked first, by her Health Visitor say, if she would like us to visit. Then if she wasn't interested we would just go away.'

'Hmph.' He was not convinced but fortunately the majority were, and we got our £2000.

The next step was to convince the other health professionals in the selected area. We invited all the health visitors and school health visitors, (as there were in those days), to tea at 4pm on a Friday afternoon. There were about twenty of the 'green ladies' as they were affectionately known, wearing their green tweed coats and green felt hats, a little like inverted chamber pots. We explained our plans with a somewhat mixed reception.

'Would you help us to identify the poorest women with large families and the most inadequate mothers for whom another pregnancy might spell disaster? Would you ask your patients if they would like a visit to discuss family planning – they would not need to attend a clinic and it would cost them nothing?'

The green ladies drank their tea and ate their biscuits and left politely two by two. I walked behind the last pair as they were leaving the room, the elder with her toes turned slightly out, reminded me, rather unkindly of a duck. She nudged her companion in the ribs with her elbow in a gesture I had only seen before in TV versions of Music Hall.

'Sex on the rates, that's all it is.'

Our invitation to the local GPs was to sherry at 5pm. Three turned up, two for political reasons. One was the chairman of the Local Medical Committee and did not practice in the area and one represented the BMA.

The third was genuinely interested in what we were hoping to do. They were very suspicious of our intentions and really wanted us to promise to ask their permission before we visited 'their' patients. We tried to emphasise that if there were fewer children in such overburdened families their doctors would have their workload reduced. It was well known that most out-of-hours visits were demanded by a very small percentage of patients on their lists and these tended to be the families who coped least well with their lives, whose children were less likely to be immunised and who were poor attenders at surgeries and clinics. We assured the GPs that we would always inform them if we were asked to visit one of their patients, especially as we would need to know if there was any medical reason why an individual patient should not use a particular method of contraception.

Superficially they were polite but our relationship with family doctors remained uneasy and was exacerbated when, in 1974, GPs were paid by the NHS to provide contraceptive services to women on their 'family planning lists'. This was a long way off in 1970 but there was a strong feeling that, by visiting patients at home, we were poaching on their preserves.

The subsequent rapid expansion of this Domiciliary Service

depended on increased funding from the City Council which would not have been forthcoming if the hard-pressed and hard-nosed Health Committee had not believed that not only were we alleviating much human misery and distress but also that there was a demonstrable economic benefit to the community.

I published a paper in the Health Bulletin in November 1974 which quantified in detail the financial savings of our intervention. It analysed the data on the first 300 women who were referred to us. Between them they had already had nearly 1500 conceptions and had borne over 1200 children, fifty of these babies were born prematurely and 44 were severely handicapped physically or mentally or both. The vulnerability of all their children continued after birth as 33 had died before our contact and there were a further eight deaths while the families were under observation. To make valid 'before and after' comparisons I worked out the total of 'women months' from first conception to contact with us and divided this by the number of conceptions during this period. This gave a 'conception rate' of one per 21.5 months. I then calculated the total number of months of contact and the number of conceptions during that time and compared this number with the predicted number if there had been no intervention. – the ratio was 30:205. The mean annual cost to the rates per domiciliary patient in 1973 was under ten pounds. The projected cost of each prevented (and unwanted) conception averaged out at £30 for their immediate medical care but when the figures were extrapolated to include the statutory financial provision for mother and child and topped up with the cost of educating 153 children who might be expected to survive, the total was around £800,00. These were the known costs but families like these are the very ones which cost the state so much because of their demands on the social services and even the police. The real figure must have been well over a million.

The eight doctors and nineteen nurses who worked in the domiciliary teams were not motivated by these sorts of considerations and the staff turnover was remarkably low. There was a great deal of job satisfaction in our work and we built up a real trust and empathy with our clients. Our main objective was to be accepted, so that we could go back at any time and be made welcome (even if half grudgingly at times). It was no part of our policy to tell people how many children they should or should not have. However heart sick we might feel for example at the desire of a retarded or unstable girl to have yet another baby to replace the one she had lost through her own incompetence, it was not for us to impose our own advice, even if we could. If we kept in touch and maintained her trust we could help her again after the child's birth.

We were concerned with helping individual families to have the number of children they wanted and we were certainly not try-ing to implement any kind of birth control policy. Those of us who had first hand knowledge of the degradation associated with real poverty felt that anything we could do to improve the quality of life for such families, especially the children, was well worth while.

Jane Docherty was twenty-five and had six children. She lived in a single-end (one room) with a cold tap in a shallow sink and shared toilet halfway down the stairs. Her sister was homeless. She had been evicted for non-payment of rent. Rather than the family being split up and the children taken into care, Jane and her husband took in Sadie, Jim and their three children. Four adults and nine children slept, ate and watched the telly in this one room. I once arrived about 10 a.m. – far too early. They were still recumbent and the door would only open sufficiently for me to squeeze in and remain standing against the wall. One couple were in the double bed 'in the wall' with a toddler beside them and another child across the foot. The other two adults lay in an extended folding settee, a six year old between them. The two babies snuggled top to tail in an old-fashioned perambulator base and the remaining children were sleeping in the two bunk beds against the wall. There was no room to walk.

'I'll come back later,' I said. By two o'clock the men were out and so were some of the children. The two women were quite happy to tell me with some pride, how they all fitted in. This situation carried on for over three months until Sadie and her family were rehoused. These sisters were the grand-daughters of a formidable matriarch who lived in Possilpark. Even then this 'scheme' had a bad reputation for crime and anti-social behaviour but drugs were not an important part of the scene in the early seventies. Mrs Graham was 68; she had eleven children, 63 grandchildren and now had 34 great grandchildren. Her eldest daughter, now in her fifties had produced 13 offspring and those who survived were well on the way to follow her example.

Tragedy and comedy walked hand in hand in the Domiciliary Service. Sometimes the humour was so obvious that there was no need to hide one's laughter. Sheila Lindsay, the Dom nurse for Blackhill, climbed three flights of stairs to 'chap' the door of one of her regulars who would soon be running out of pills.

'Is Effie in?'

The unshaven man who answered the door replied, 'Naw, she's awa doon at her maw's.'

'Tell her I called.'

'Oh, aye.'

She toiled back the following week, this time she was 'awa at the factor's'. Subsequent visits produced 'doing the messages' and 'up at the scule'. After two months Sheila was concerned that wherever her errant client was, she must definitely have run out of her oral contraceptives. As always she did not give up and she was finally rewarded when Effie herself opened the door.

'Oh, there you are Effie, where have you been?'

'Och, I was lifted by the polis fur shoplifting. I've been in Corntonvale (the women's prison).'

'Well I wish your man had told me. I've worn my shoe leather out climbing these stairs.'

As quick as a flash came the reply, 'What size do you take? Ah'll get ye a pair next time Ah'm oot.'

Shoplifting was a normal way of life. The women worked in twos or more often threes, not going to Glasgow but to the satellite towns round about such as Motherwell, Hamilton and Coatbridge. They would concentrate on the big chain stores such as M&S, BHS and Littlewoods. They took orders from their friends for specific items – a red anorak for a boy of ten, jeans for a fifteen year old and so on. One of the party had an old banger of a car in which they set off about 10 a.m. and they would be back before noon with the loot. Items which were not earmarked were sold off at half price in a 'house sale' in the afternoon. Every now and then one of the team was caught but they regarded the two months in 'the jail' (three month sentence, one off for good behaviour) as a risk worth taking.

A recently delivered grand multipara (a lady who had had more than six deliveries) was referred to me by the Royal Maternity Hospital at Rotten Row. She was due to go back into hospital to be sterilised when the baby was three months old and neither she nor the obstetric staff wanted any more little mistakes to occur in the interval. She had had a bad time over this most recent birth, her eighth. The family were squatting in a condemned tenement in Black Street opposite the V.D. clinic.

One wet Wednesday I went across the road in my lunch hour. The terrace of four storey flats looked long abandoned. The roof had several obvious holes where the slates had come off; there was no glass in the lower windows and not much at higher levels where some windows were boarded up and others covered by sacking. It was impossible to make out the house numbers but one street door was slightly ajar. I went in and started climbing the worn stone stair, wishing that the remains of the wooden handrail were more substantial. I was reminded of a similar foray into another condemned tenement where the Health Visitor had advised, 'Take torch (no light) and brick (to throw at rats).'

I climbed carefully to the second floor, eight steps up, turn on the half landing, then eight more. I started up the last flight, my rubber-soled shoes making no noise on the treads. As I came up to the turn I was astonished to see a man reading the Pink 'Un as he sat enthroned on the lavatory. I don't know who was the more surprised but I am sure he was the most disconcerted. To be found by a lady with your trousers round your ankles and be unable to rise to the occasion must be a cause for embarrassment to any gentleman.

'I've come to see your wife. Is she up the stair?'

'Oh, aye.' I went on up. Sure enough the rest of the family were living in a two-roomed apartment on the top floor. The new baby lay in an old wheel-less Silver Cross pram whose hood remained up to keep out the rain. The water was leaking through a hole in the roof and trickling down the electric flex in the middle of the ceiling from which depended a bare sixty watt bulb. This provided some much needed light as one of the two windows was boarded up. The other five surviving children, (one had died of gastro-enteritis the year before) were playing and fighting in varying degrees of semi-nakedness in the cramped space remaining after a folding settee and a bunk had been accommodated. There was no covering on the floor, not even linoleum. The younger ones exhibited the 'bare bottoms on bare boards' syndrome I associated with extreme poverty. Nappies were expensive – washing and then drying six or seven a day was virtually impossible without running, let alone hot, water. As soon as a baby stopped crawling or bottom shuffling his nether regions were left exposed and he peed or defaecated onto the bare boards which might or might not have newspaper over the most vulnerable areas. Once semi-continent he went into trousers, frequently with no top although a ragged T-shirt was put on in winter.

I did not wonder that the progenitor of the surrounding mayhem had escaped to a more private and quieter place. Mrs Fallon gladly agreed to take the pill for three months. I called again about six weeks later to check that she had not changed her mind about the operation and that she had no problems with her contraception. All was well from that point of view and I was glad to see that the rain was now diverted away from the light fixture by a piece of guttering that had been pushed diagonally through the ceiling plaster to collect the water directly and then allow it to fall vertically into a bucket.

That was the last time I saw the Fallons as I had a letter from Rotten Row soon after informing me that she had had her tubes tied without any complications and no longer needed the services of the Domiciliary Service.

More Sex on the Rates

Shortly before my retirement when drug abuse was an increasingly desperate problem I was asked to visit a seventeen year old girl who had dropped out of a rehabilitation programme. She was thought to be living with her boyfriend in a tower block near the Citizen's Theatre. I did not manage to make the visit until around five o'clock one Saturday. I always lost my way south of the river but at least in this case, I could see where I was supposed to be making for and there was no difficulty in parking my mini. I found the only working lift and reluctantly stepped in, pressing the button for the eleventh floor. It smelt of urine and vomit and, in addition to the ubiquitous graffiti, there were smears of unmentionable substances on the walls. I did not like being in a lift in such a tower block. If a drunk or aggressive character got in, one was locked up with him (and it was the 'hims' I was wary of) for the duration of the journey and the ascent could be fearfully slow. As I got out. I saw a pale face looking out from a partially opened door.

'I'm looking for Julie. Can you tell me which is her door?' As I asked him the question I could see that the scruffy youth looked extremely ill.

'What's the matter? I'm a doctor. You look as though you are going to faint.'

'She's gone to get an ambulance. I was hoping she'd be back. . .'

I sat him down, indeed he would have fallen otherwise. And then I pieced the story together. He had been in a knife fight ten days before and had been admitted to the Royal Infirmary with a deep stab wound which had cut his popliteal artery, the main blood vessel behind the knee. It was repaired but he was kept in hospital for nearly a week and was discharged to Julie's care. They were preparing to go out for a fish supper when he suddenly felt a severe pain in his chest and became very short of breath. They both realised he was seriously ill and she had gone out to phone an ambulance. First she had tried banging on the doors of the other flats on their landing but no-one would open their door and she decided to try and find a phone in the street. She had not been living with Paul for long and they had no friends locally. In those days before mobiles, trying to find a working telephone in such an area was a nightmare. Public kiosks were few and all were vandalised. She returned fifteen minutes later, sobbing and desperate. Later she told me that when she went out again she eventually found a phone and dialled 999 for the ambulance service. They told her that as Paul had been taken ill at home they could do nothing until his general practitioner called them. Julie shouted that he did not have a GP and that he was very ill. It made no difference – I am sure she used some pretty abusive language in her desperation and that would not have helped.

I looked at Paul. He was deathly pale and sweating. His pulse was racing along at over 100 beats a minute and he was very breathless. I was certain he had had a pulmonary embolism, a clot of blood shooting up from the injured vessel in his leg to lodge in his lung. It had obviously been a large one and if he had another it would probably be fatal. I thought of the problems of going myself to find a phone, convincing the ambulance service and waiting while they responded, leaving these two seventeen year olds alone while he possibly died. The practical solution was to take him to Casualty in the mini but first we had to get him to the lift and then into the car when we reached the bottom. I still remember the agonising slowness of that descent. It seemed to stop at every one of the intervening ten floors while Julie and I supported Paul between us as he leant back in a corner of the cage. Somehow we got him into the car, Julie in behind, and I drove through the early evening traffic to the ambulance bay outside the A&E department at the Royal. I jumped out and went straight to find a porter who could collect Paul in a wheelchair, and then on to locate someone in authority who would listen and appreciate the urgency of the case. As soon as I said he had only recently been discharged from the vascular surgery unit they took notice and he was safely handed over to the experts while Julie gave his particulars to Reception.

I retired soon after this but heard from a colleague who took over Julie's contraceptive needs, that Paul made a good recovery from his embolism but that neither had been able to give up their drug habit.

Cathie McNally was expecting her seventh child. She was already about seven months pregnant but had managed to avoid any antenatal care. She had a phobia about being examined 'down below' by a man. Even the normal palpation of the abdomen by a member of the male sex was repugnant to her. All her babies had been 'delivered' at home – BBAs as the jargon went ('born before arrival' – at the hospital) – except the last, when even she had not been able to avoid admission. Her waters broke when she was seeking a bargain at the 'Barras' Market one Sunday morning. The immediate concern of her fellow shoppers resulted in the swift arrival of an ambulance and the delivery of her sixth infant under the roof of the Royal Maternity Hospital. This fortuitous intervention undoubtedly saved the baby's life as the cord was wound tightly round her neck and only the skilled action of the midwife prevented her being stillborn.

This time I had tried to convince Cathie that there was a real risk both to the child and herself unless she had some antenatal care. I had arranged with the hospital for her to be seen when there was a female registrar on duty at the clinic. She agreed that I could pick her up at 10 a.m. and take her to Rotten Row (the local name for a much loved institution). It was no use fixing an earlier time, even 10 a.m. was pushing it a bit. I was not surprised when, on chapping her door, it was opened by a skinny waif of six or so who told me, 'Ma Maw's oot.'

Undeterred I walked through the close into the backcourt. I didn't think Cathie would have gone far. Sure enough, there she was smoking a quick fag beside the bins, but at least she had her coat on and was wearing shoes, not slippers. She came with me, resigned and only asking when she was settled in the car if she could smoke another fag 'for her nerves'. I willingly agreed but she had to put it out before we went into the Antenatal Clinic.

As always, Sister Rappa was unfazed by our late arrival. After Cathie's particulars had been completed and her blood pressure taken, she was escorted to one of a row of cubicles. She was asked to undress and put on a short hospital gown that opened down the back. These small dressing rooms were entered from the rear and a second door opened directly into the examination room. Cathie's name was duly called but, instead of coming out, she shot out of the back, through reception and into the street wearing only her hospital gown with her clothes clutched under her arm. Half the pupil midwives in Rotten Row followed her down the hill. She ran remarkably fast considering the gradient of Montrose Street and the advanced stage of her pregnancy. She managed to hail a taxi in George Square before the chasing pack caught up with her. Six weeks later she was safely delivered in the labour ward in spite of her protests. Her husband had decided it was time he made the decisions in the household and had escorted her into the hospital by taxi until it was too late for her to escape. I won't say he had not been influenced by a few words from me into his ear.

Some of the patients we were asked to help were so inadequate, so vulnerable and so much at the mercy of anyone or any event which touched them that one felt that helping them to control their fertility was almost the only positive step that could be taken. They were like little paper boats, just staying afloat, tossing about on the ocean of life but quite unable to control the direction in which they were going. Almost all deprived young women want a baby. Our objective with fourteen and fifteen year olds was to try and defer the first conception until they were a little older. We did not always succeed but motherhood at seventeen was better than motherhood four years earlier.

We had several referrals of very young mothers following delivery who were now back in the community. Twin sisters of fifteen each gave birth to a baby within a fortnight of one another. One went home to Mum and the other went to live with her boyfriend's family. Both had beautiful long Titian red hair and both were unable to read more than the simplest words. I visited Anna first and, with Mother's help had no difficulty in starting her on the pill. Next, to Netta: I rattled the letter-box and the door was opened by a slight skinny boy of about twelve. Like her sister, Netta did not want to have another baby 'just yet'. She decided to have the injection because she knew she would forget to take her tablet every night. After our immediate business was completed I had time to look round. The mantelpiece was covered with cards. At first sight I thought these were congratulations on the arrival of her daughter but then I realised they were birthday cards.

'I didn't know you had just had a birthday,' I said.

'Naw, naw, it's ma man.'

The lad I had taken to be a younger brother spoke up.

'They're mine. Ah wiz fourteen last Sa'urday so we've only got tae wait fur two years afore we cin get mairrit.'

I tracked another young homeless girl to a squat in a condemned tenement in the Gorbals. In 1971 this was the old notorious Glasgow slum before it was razed to the ground and rebuilt with such high hopes and good intentions by Sir Basil Spence. (His buildings have already gone the way of their predecessors and yet a third Gorbals has now risen from the rubble.) I climbed the broken flight of steps up to the open door of the close and found Janey sitting on an orange box with some other poor women round a fire of what looked like broken chair legs and packing cases.

'Hallo, I've come to see Janey. I'm from the Family Planning.'

She looked up but made no move, her white face blotched with crying.

'Perhaps we could go somewhere more private?' She stood up and led the way into another room with mattresses almost touching each other covering the floor. Janey indicated the only chair and squatted down on a mattress.

'Is one of the others looking after your baby?'

She started crying with her hands over her face, rocking backwards and forwards in total misery.

'What's the matter?' I asked.

'The wean's deid.'

'Whatever happened?' I asked.

'They said it wiz a cot death.'

Slowly she became more composed and less tense and started telling me her story. She was seventeen and had been brought up 'in care' (the true meaning of the phrase is just the opposite – without care and certainly without love). It was inevitable that she should go with the first man who offered to live with her when she was given a flat, a little furniture and told to get on with it as soon as she turned sixteen. It was no surprise that he abandoned her when she found she was pregnant. He had 'looked after' her money, she could not pay the rent and she ended up on the streets, pregnant and friendless. She had lied to the hospital, pretending she still lived at her old address as she was afraid she would be sent to a Mother and Baby Home. This would probably have been her salvation as the two I often visited were both comfortable and compassionate but she had heard stories about the babies being forcibly 'taken off' the young mothers and she dreaded being sent to one. So she had ended up in this 'women's refuge', a condemned squat without even the basic amenities which was all there was in those days before the involvement of the Social Services.

She and her baby shared the same thin mattress and two blankets but, as she explained, 'the wean woudnae stop his greetin'. She was afraid that the other women would be annoyed and would 'put her oot' so 'Ah jist put oot ma haun' an smothered him.'

In the morning she was discovered cradling the tiny dead infant and her flatmates assumed that the child had been 'overlain', a common lay diagnosis before the publicity associated with 'cot death' or Sudden Infant Death Syndrome. The authorities had officially taken the SIDS line. She had told nobody what really happened.

I did nothing. What good would it have done? Even if she were charged on the strength of a confession she would have been charged with infanticide, not murder. A conviction would only have resulted in probation for one of her youth and poor comprehension. In this respect the law of the United Kingdom is light years ahead of the United States. As for wretched Janey, it was before Depo-Provera was available and she had an IUD fitted. It was not the ideal method because of the risks associated with infection especially if she went back on the streets, but we both knew she would never remember to take a pill every night. Some of the other women in the refuge were kindly enough and did their best to keep an eye on her but I felt Janey was one of life's born losers.

Mrs McGinley lived on the Barrowfield, in my opinion the most lawless and violent of all the wretched housing schemes in Glasgow. It lay between the Milanda bakery on London Road and the Gallowgate, almost adjoining the Celtic football ground at Parkhead.

It was small in area but concentrated in vice and it was inviting certain trouble to leave one's car in Stamford or Dalserf Street. The management at Milanda had been very helpful when I asked if I could leave my Mini inside their well-protected compound while I did my visits round the corner and this was my normal practice. On this occasion I had only the one visit to make and I decided to risk parking outside the close to save the bother of checking in with the gateman, finding a space and then walking round to Mrs McGinley's.

She lived Three Up Left and I trudged up the filthy stairs with her notes under my arm and my 'Dom bag' held in my other hand, bulging with contraceptive supplies, blood pressure machine, stethoscope and medicaments likely to be needed by my female clients. She was a very large lady, the rolls of fat unconstrained by any under garment. She always wore black. Whether this was token mourning for the absence of her husband who spent most of his adult life in prison, with brief interludes in which he had fathered ten children, or whether she thought black was 'her colour', I don't know. She was always friendly and cooperative and had not had a pregnancy for over three years.

I was calling because she had left a message to say she had run out of pills. As she explained when I arrived slightly breathless at her door, 'Ah hadnae reelly run oot. Ma Man put them on the fire when he wiz lifted (by the police).'

She did not volunteer why he had been remanded in custody – it was better not to know in the Barrowfield. Nor did I enquire why she needed the pill now her consort had departed. I was pleased that she had enough confidence in the Dom to get in touch and to tell me the truth of the situation (probably).

When I got up to go she resumed her usual stance, 'hingin' oot the windy', leaning out, her massive forearms supported by a dirty cushion on the bottom sill of the open window. As I started down the stairs I heard a sound I knew all too well – glass breaking and tinkling onto the tarmac. As I came out of the close I saw at once that a metal fence post had been driven through one of the rear side windows of the Mini. Closer inspection showed that it had been done with such force that the metal of the panel on the opposite side had been dented out. The bag with all the case notes for my visits that day had gone. There was nothing else to take.

As a policeman in Barrowfield had once said to me, 'The kids round here would smash your windscreen for a packet of cigarettes.' I had hoped that as I never left anything in the vehicle,(no car radios in those days) and I did not smoke, I would escape vandalism. I should have known better. This was the third time I had had a window smashed in this scheme. It never happened to me in Blackhill where I had worked much longer.

I glanced up at Mrs McGinley looking out like a great black toad from the top of a rock. I knew perfectly well who had been responsible.

'Mrs McGinley, if I don't get my bag back with all my patients notes in it, the whole scheme is going to know your private business.'

She was immediately galvanised into action.

'Joseph, Thomas, Frankie, find the doctor's bag for her at once.' Three or four grinning urchins appeared from nowhere.

'Please, Missus, I know which way he went. Follae me.' The nine year old led the way into the next close and up the stairs. Halfway up the second flight there was the nearly empty bag, its contents spilled down the steps. It had only contained case notes which had no value for these boys, who had abandoned the lot as worthless. I gathered them up and went down to the Mini.

'Wees'll help ye. We ken fine what tae dae.' They certainly did, they had plenty of practice. The doors were opened, the seat cushion on the back seat tipped up and the floor carpeting lifted out so that most of the shattered glass could be tipped into the gutter. Meanwhile another brother had peeled the rubber squab from the broken window, emptied the remaining shards and carefully fitted it back. It was all done in five minutes.

'Thank you for your help, boys,' I said as I drove away to have the window replaced. It was no good getting annoyed. The incident was part of the job and had not been without its ironic humour.

In spite of the violence and crime among the people we visited there were very few incidents in which domiciliary staff were in real danger. This has changed now I understand but up to 1990 when I left, it was our vehicles rather than our persons that were at risk.

I was only really scared once and that was literally by a mad woman with an axe. She had been referred by the staff at Rotten Row. She was a chronic schizophrenic who had recently been delivered of her third child who had immediately been taken into care, as had its predecessors. She had expressed no interest in the baby and did not seem to notice, let alone care, when the child was taken away. She had gone back to live with her partner in one of the few remaining old mid-nineteenth century tenements near the Saltmarket. The flats were on landings with a common outside stair housed in a rectangular 'tower' connected to each level by a bridge spanning the underlying footpath. I believe this had been a common design but this was the only place I had come across it. I found the right apartment with some difficulty. I was only sure I was right when I knocked repeatedly on the unpainted door and it was partially opened by the living Witch of Endor. The emaciated white face, edentulous jaws and long straggly unkempt grey hair made her look more sixty than forty. I explained the reason for my visit but she was reluctant to admit me until a man's voice said, 'Och, jist let her in.'

Inside the single room it was dark, the window covered by sacking and the little light came from a small fire of wood. They were each sitting on an orange box and there were several partially dismembered boxes lying about. Our conversation did not go well. My attempts to point out the benefits of avoiding a further conception fell on deaf ears. Neither were interested. Then, suddenly she became angry.

'It's nae bizness of yours. Get oot and dinnae come back.'

I did not hesitate but was not quick enough for her and she picked up a large axe – it was no little chopper – and advanced. I got out of the door as fast as I could, shutting it behind me. I almost ran across the 'drawbridge' to the relative safety of the stairwell. Then to my horror I heard the door open and she stood there, wielding the axe in both hands.

'An when Ah sez dinnae come back, Ah mean **niver**.'

She went inside and slammed the door. I had to report one of my few failures to Sister Rappa.

Waiting for the Pram Park

Blackhill was a typical council housing scheme only two miles north and east of the city centre. It had been built a few years before the war to re-house families suffering from tuberculosis from the old slum tenements . They were supposed to benefit from the fresh air of its relatively elevated situation and the open spaces round it. Three gasometers marked the western boundary and thirty years later much larger 'schemes' enclosed it on the other three sides. The tenements were basically sound and all had a bathroom, inside lavatory and a kitchenette with cooker and potentially hot running water. The four storey blocks had an open passage or 'close' running through into the backcourt between every second ground floor flat, that gave access to the stairs and the six flats above. There were many households where nobody was gainfully employed, but some women had a job – petrol pump attendant, poorly paid machine operator or a clippy (conductress) on the buses.

Not infrequently patients from Black Street became clients in Blackhill. Not long after I started in the Glasgow V.D. department a thin undersized young girl in the last stages of pregnancy had somehow got herself to the clinic just before we closed for lunch. It was the end of my shift and a very hot day. She had gonorrhoea and needed a penicillin injection.

'Naw, naw, Ah'm feart o' jags. Leave me alane.' She was trembling with fear and was only restrained from running away with considerable difficulty.

'Come on Agnes, it's not really sore. It'll be over in less than a minute,' but she would not be comforted. We could give her tablets but this was less satisfactory because one dose was not enough and we doubted her ability to take the rest. In any case this was also to prove a non-starter.

'Ah cannae swallow pills. They get stuck in ma throat.'

'Where does she live?,' I asked Margaret.

'Acrehill Street.'

'Where's that?'

'Blackhill,' said Sister Anderson in a tone which said 'that explains everything'.

'Where's that?' I asked.

'It's off the main road to Edinburgh beyond the Fruit Market.' I had a vague idea.

'Look I'm going out that way now so I could take her home.'

'Oh no, Doctor. **You** couldn't possibly go into Blackhill.' The faces were shocked.

'Why not? You go there contact tracing and health visitors work there.'

I turned to the sniffling girl.

'Agnes, if I gave you a lift home in my motor would you have your jag?'

This was enough to tip the scales and gripping both my hands tightly, she allowed Sister Anderson to give her the injection.

I asked for directions, fortunately it was only about a mile and once on familiar territory my now cheerful but still very hot and pregnant passenger directed me to her 'maw's hoose'. In those days private cars were uncommon in the schemes and there was a lot of prestige in arriving home in one, even if it was only a Mini.

This was my first introduction to Blackhill or any of the other virtually identical housing estates of Glasgow. It was grey and dirty, with rank grass poking up between the filthy litter and dog turds in the unpaved strips of earth in front of the windows.

'Hooray, Hooray, the IRA' confronted 'Fuck the Micks' on any spare wall and packs of marauding dogs restlessly hunted across the streets and round the blocks.

Three years later I caught up with Agnes. She had had two more children since our first meeting but she felt she needed a rest. Three children before she was twenty were already more than she could manage and she was relieved to know that someone would visit her at home to provide what she needed.

'Ah cannae even go on a bus wi' three weans. It's nae guid me saying Ah'll get tae the clinic. Ah cannae. It's no that Ah want anither yin, ken, but what can Ah dae? Ma man's goat tae have his rights. It's no fur me tae tell him naw.'

At that time there was no clinic in Blackhill. There was a Health Visitors' station, a first floor flat up a close in the middle of the scheme. When the Domiciliary Service expanded to include the whole city north of the river, the local green lady (the Health Visitor), was a very devout Catholic and much opposed to our activities. It was rumoured that if she saw us coming out of a close she would ask the priest to sprinkle it with Holy Water. While this was probably apocryphal, it was true that she asked him to visit any woman whom she knew we had been advising. As she was an excellent health visitor from every other viewpoint, her all-seeing presence did inhibit our clients especially if they were Catholics. After some months the problem was solved by the good lady being moved to another area where she was part of a team and her personal influence was less apparent. At the time I knew nothing of the behind-the-scenes machinations which resulted in her transfer. We were just delighted to welcome two replacements who were enthusiastic supporters of family planning.

Their 'station' was small and there was no space for an examination couch in addition to the large desk in the main room. Four chairs were lined up in the passage from the only door. There were supposed to be not more than six persons in the flat at the same time because of fire regulations. I would have complied with these more rigorously if there had not been a connecting door through the wall to the adjacent flat occupied by a Barnardo's Toddlers Group.

Some of the women who told their health visitor that they wanted family planning were unhappy about the Domiciliary staff coming to their houses, usually because their husbands (or sometimes their mothers-in-law) were thought to be against it. They all had to call at the Health Visitors' office to collect dried milk for their babies and to ask for advice about feeding problems and minor ailments. If they called on Tuesday mornings, Margaret Wallace and I would be there to discuss their contraceptive needs and, nearly always, to give them what they wanted. The IUD was frequently the method of choice as husbands could not find it (and perhaps burn it, as sometimes happened with the pill). We spread a blanket covered by a sheet of plastic and a roll of paper towel, on the desk and used that as an examination couch, not only for inserting coils but also to diagnose pregnancies, take swabs from discharges and generally act as a minor gynaecology clinic.

In due course more suitable premises were created by converting two ground floor flats across the road into one long clinic. We eagerly awaited the opening day but there were repeated delays. I contacted the Chief Administrative Nursing Officer who was the ultimate boss of the Health Visitors and whom I knew to be an ally.

'What on earth is holding it up?'

'You'll not believe this,' said Miss Nairn. 'The architects and the building department cannot agree about the size of the pram park!'

As none of the mothers in Blackhill owned a pram and would

not have dreamt of leaving their precious buggies outside any clinic, however architecturally meritorious the shelter provided, this was the ultimate in bureaucratic futility. We moved in eventually without the pram park and the mums brought their buggies into the clinic with them.

By that time most of the population of the scheme knew who we were and what we did. My Mini and Margaret's Metro were recognised at once. In the early days we had to earn the respect of the community and we were asked some funny questions. Crossing the road one morning about half past ten (hardly anybody was up before then) I was hailed from an upper window by a cheeky-faced boy of nine or so.

'Hey, Missus, are youse frae the scule board?' Those were the days when truancy officers called on the families of persistent offenders. Whether they were any more successful than present-day social workers, I have no idea.

A vest-clad man leaned out of his top floor window and called down to Sister Wallace, 'Missus, Missus, is youse the pill wuman?'

She called back, 'Yes, that's me.'

'Well ma wife needs ye.'

'Which house is it?'

'Three up, left.'

'I'll be along in half an hour or so.'

We were known as the 'pill women' for many years and felt proud to be christened into the Blackhill community.

The converted ground floor flats in Acrehill Street that comprised the clinic (minus a pram park) were multi-purpose. A door opened into the close at either end but one of these was normally kept locked. Above were four flats on two levels whose inhabitants were already well-known to the staff. Three year old John Paul, born at the time of the Papal visit to Glasgow, subsequently fulfilled the expectations resting in his family by climbing on the roof of Sally's new vehicle and scoring its circumference with a broken glass lemonade bottle. His mother said the child had to play somewhere and she was far too busy to watch him all the time.

The premises were open every day from nine in the morning until about four-thirty in the afternoon. Our family planning session was on Tuesdays from twelve until mid-afternoon, with a brief break for coffee between 1.30 and 2.0 when the waiting room emptied for the TV serial *Neighbours* as most of our clients lived within five minutes buggy push from their own homes. Speech therapy, chiropody and, of course baby clinics, occupied most of the rest of the week. Two closes along was the sandbagged police station and a small general shop heavily defended with wire mesh and a minimal amount of window. Our doors had outer covers of steel and the windows were fitted with specially toughened glass. Even this was broken and it had to be further reinforced. After that the local lads found other methods of breaking in. One successful approach was through the floor, making a hole into the raised brick foundations and then getting inside by pushing up the manhole cover which provided access to the service ducts. The fitted floor covering made little difference to the ease with which they pushed it open. On that occasion we only lost articles which were small enough to go through the trap door, but when the flat above became empty the thieves moved in before the Council had secured the door. This time they came through the ceiling and took larger items. The police, reportedly playing cards at the time and reluctant to interrupt their game, observed the fridge being carried across the road into one of the flats opposite. True or not the 'polis' had no difficulty locating the stolen goods in the morning and charging the offenders.

The two health visitors were young women, totally dedicated to their lawless patch, tough with the scroungers but having great understanding and empathy with their poverty-stricken clients. They knew exactly who was feuding with whom, which women were beaten by their useless menfolk, which children were at risk because of their mother's addiction to alcohol (drugs were to come later) and sometimes more dangerous knowledge. Murder was not uncommon and the whole community generally knew the perpetrator. Sometimes the two families, the victim's and the killer's were close neighbours and witnesses were unlikely to testify. Jean saw her brother stabbed to death outside her window and was the prime witness for the prosecution. She was moved away from the neighbourhood for nearly a year while the accused man was held in custody pending trial in the High Court of Glasgow. On the first day she was due to give her evidence she went to the ladies toilet in the basement of the building and there she was set upon. Beaten with a rolled umbrella, she was kicked within inches of her life by the mother and sisters of the murderer. The force of the blows ruptured her spleen and it was only the proximity of the Royal Infirmary that saved her life.

Vandalism was the rule but neither Margaret Wallace, her successor Sheila Lindsay, nor I, ever had any damage done to our cars in Blackhill. I don't think this was entirely due to the protective prowess of some of the small boys who offered to 'watch yer motor fur ye, Missus'. There was one particular waif-like urchin who looked no more than five or six but whom I knew to be at least eight, who would be waiting by the side of the Mini when I emerged from a close. His short trousers were too long, held up by string over his shoulders and he always wore a man's cloth cap back to front, the peak hanging down between his chicken wing shoulder blades.

'Please Missus, will ye gie us a wee hurl?' He had waited, sometimes for over half an hour, just for the chance of a 500 yard ride in a motor car. I expect his sons might now be jump-starting cars and joyriding along the M8.

The Start of the Troubles

My friendship with Dr Joyce Neill dates exactly from the start of 'The Troubles' in Northern Ireland in 1972. She had moved to Belfast in the early sixties when family planning kept a low profile. The Women's Welfare Clinic founded and manned by dedicated volunteers provided a caring if limited service. Joyce burst into this rather clubby, cosy, unambitious scene and fairly shook it up. She was intelligent, caring, motivated, articulate and energetic. She was given a small sum to set up another clinic on the other side of the city (perhaps to get her out of their hair!). This proved a great success and fulfilled an obvious need.

Joyce held an English Family Planning Association certificate and one by one the discomfited other doctors, muttering about unnecessary trouble and expense, went off to London to substantiate their credentials. She forged an excellent relationship with the University Obstetric and Gynaecology department and family planning clinics were established in both the Royal Maternity and the Belfast City Hospitals. She was greatly interested in training both undergraduates and clinical medical officers and, in 1968, invited the Medical Director of the FPA, Dr Hilary Hill, to visit Northern Ireland and assess the senior doctors with a view to their becoming Trainers.

In order to have parity of esteem with training in the rest of the UK it was necessary for the premises to be inspected as well. I had been the Chairman of the Clinic Doctors National Council over the past two years and had been reaccredited as an 'Instructing Doctor' that year, so was selected by the FPA together with Mrs Lamb, a senior nurse, to assess six clinics jointly with Dr Neill and a nursing colleague. Our visit coincided with the first Loyalist backlash to IRA violence. There was a general strike, power supplies were cut off, transport paralysed and petrol, milk and bread ran out. Every clinic was visited where the staff presented themselves for work despite the difficulties and some danger. One nurse apologised for being late because a bomb had gone off in the car park where she had left her vehicle while she did some shopping on her way to work.

We were due to visit the clinic in Portadown one evening. The name was to become notorious, but I heard it on the eight a.m. news for the first time. There had been angry confrontations overnight and Joyce's husband, Desmond, was concerned for our safety. We had a hospital clinic to visit first in the morning and as we drove off Joyce realised that although she was presently in no danger of running out of petrol, she did not have enough to take us on a round trip to Portadown.

'Must remember to fill up at my usual garage on the way home,' she remarked. On our return we pulled into the forecourt of the almost deserted petrol station.

'I'm sorry Dr Neill, I can't serve you. You know the power is off?'

'Yes, I heard this morning there was to be a general strike by Loyalists which might affect the electricity supply. I suppose that's the reason? But haven't you got some kind of manual pump which we could use?'

'I'm sorry Dr Neill but it's as much as my life is worth to serve you. I had three of the heavy mob here about an hour ago when they realised I was serving my customers with the hand pump. Threatened to blow up the place and me with it if I didn't go along with them.'

We drove thoughtfully home.

When Desmond realised we were determined to go to Portadown he reluctantly did his best to help. Detaching the hose from the washing machine he tried to suck petrol from the tank of his much loved Citroen in an attempt to siphon the fuel into Joyce's car. The calibre of the pipe was too great and his reward was a mouthful of petrol, which was still perceptible on his breath even after cleaning his teeth and the liberal use of a mouthwash. Poor Des, he was going out later to give an address at a student function. The Chairman smoked heavily and Des had visions of an explosion which might blow them all off the platform.

Des and Joyce were both committed Friends and Quaker couples hold all their worldly goods in common but some things are held more in common than others. Although Des had owned the Citroen for more than two years, his wife had only driven it once. Admittedly the fact that the gear lever was fixed to the steering column was a factor in her lack of practice but Des did have reservations about allowing someone so inexperienced to drive it. In spite of these qualms he handed over the keys and apprehensively waved us goodbye. As we set out in the dark and wet, Joyce said, 'I'll concentrate on the driving and you watch out for road blocks.'

About five miles short of Portadown we pulled into a lay-by, as had been arranged. There, one of the local clinic staff was waiting for us. Her car drove off and we followed, soon leaving the dual carriageway and bearing left down a secondary road. We arrived at a country house where several vehicles were parked in the driveway. We transferred into a Volvo Estate which transported us and three other clinic workers over a bridge several miles upstream from the town. In this way we reached our destination from the south without having to cross the main bridge in the town centre, the scene of the violence of the night before. Naturally there were hardly any patients but all the staff were present and Joyce and I and Mrs Lamb and her colleague felt that the time we were able to spend asking about clinical practices, inspecting the premises and examining case notes was an adequate test of their competence.

The other inspection which stuck in my memory was in Newtonards Road. The premises were in the ground floor of a gloomy building on the corner of a main road and a side street. Cars were parked nose to tail in front and we had to find a space in the side road. Again, the staff were all present but there were no patients. There was a feeling of apprehension and we were all a bit edgy and tense, waiting for something to happen, we hardly knew what. Then we became aware of steadily increasing noise, drum beats, whistles, shouts and marching feet. It was so overwhelming that we could not hear conversation inside the room while it passed. The windows were covered with fixed curtains but had old-fashioned quarter lights at the top. We stood on two examination couches arranged along the wall under the windows and watched the march go past. A solid human snake, six abreast engulfed the street. Those nearest us were not confined to the pavement but stamped along the roofs and bonnets of the parked cars, thumping the metal with staves and poles from which waved the Bloody Hand of Ulster to encourage the laggards. The terrifying thing about that parade was that so many were children – boys, I saw no females in that mob, some as young as eight or nine and hundreds who could not have been more than thirteen. This was the Protestant March on Stormont and the beginning of nearly thirty years of violence generated by the hatreds of the past.

I stayed with Joyce and Desmond several times after that memorable week until in 1986 a bomb went off in the road outside their house in a quiet residential street. A judge lived next door but his wife was ill and he was visiting her in hospital. Desmond had gone out in the car to do the weekly shopping as they had both retired some years before. Joyce was in the kitchen at the back when the explosion shattered the windows and brought plaster down from the ceiling. A large hole was blown in the roof of the house whose garden backed onto theirs in the road behind. Shock has a strange effect on humans as well as property. She remembers going to the cupboard and fetching a dustpan and brush to sweep up the mess! When she tried to leave the house she could not open the front door and went into the garden to escape round the side of the house but the bomb had set light to the hedge and front gate and she was trapped until rescued by a fireman. Their house needed five months of repair and renovation to make it habitable again. During this time the university rented them a very small postgraduate flat. It consisted of two rooms, the kitchenette being partially partitioned off from the living room. The bedroom only just accommodated a double bed with a small bedside chair on either side.

When I went to visit them a mutual friend very kindly offered me hospitality in her lovely country house and then drove me into the city to spend the day with the Neills. Somehow the sight of these two elderly people displaced from their own home and uncomplainingly coping with considerable discomforts made me feel more anger than the knowledge of murders and atrocities inflicted on other innocent victims. There was no room for their books in the tiny flat, which were stored in trunks and boxes in the cellar of the house in Cadogan Park. Separation from their library was the most trying hardship but after five months they were able to return home. I was working during these years and could only visit Belfast over a weekend. This enabled me to go to 'Meeting' with Joyce and gave me some small idea of the workings of The Society of Friends. I think if I had any religious belief I would identify most closely with their doctrines (or lack of them) but I would find it almost impossible to live my life according to their self-denying principles. They have intellectualised religion and discarded most of the irrational dogma I find so repugnant.

'It's Downright Disgusting'

My introduction to Lennox Castle and the world of the mentally handicapped came through Black Street. Mamie was seventeen and had hitch-hiked up to Scotland from Bradford where she had run away from her brother's house. She had lived virtually as a slave, despised and rejected by her strict Muslim family because she was of mixed race and her mother had committed suicide after the disgrace of giving birth. The police in Glasgow city centre had picked her up, homeless, hungry and dirty. When it became evident that she was of limited intelligence they had shipped her off to the huge mental deficiency institution, Lennox Castle, fifteen miles to the north. She arrived at Black Street by ambulance with a nursing escort for 'a check-up', much as the women prisoners were brought from Corntonvale. She was terrified, trembling and mute and could barely be persuaded to sit on the chair beside my desk.

'Thank you, nurse. There is no need for you to stay in the room.'

'Oh, but I must. Dr Brown told me to stay with her at all times in case she ran away.'

'Well, I'm the doctor here and I can manage very well. If you go back to reception I'm sure someone will find you a cup of tea.'

With a snort of protest the jailer nurse left the room.

'Now, Mamie, tell me a wee bit about yourself.'

Gradually the story emerged and, as she relaxed she sat back in the chair and stopped hugging herself. I modified my voice a little to suit her Yorkshire accent.

'So what did you do when you found yourself in Glasgow?'

'I was that hungry I let a bloke go wi' me for a bag o' chips. I was trying to kip down over a grating like, 'cos it was warm but the police picked me up.'

'What about your family?'

She immediately stiffened. 'Nay, nay, I can't go back. They'd kill me. Any road, I don't know the address and I wouldn't tell even if I did.'

I explained that I would have to examine her but that I would be very gentle and one of our nurses would be there to hold her hand. She eventually agreed to this as long as the nurse from Lennox Castle was not allowed in.

When it was done I asked, 'Why didn't you want that nurse in here?'

'It's a terrible place that, Doctor. They lock you up on your own if you disobey the rules. They just treat you like dirt. I hate it.'

'Well I'm afraid you'll have to go back for now but we'll have to do some more tests in a few days and I'll see you again then.'

I was very disturbed when, a week later, the same poker-faced nurse came into the clinic and asked for help to bring Mamie from the ambulance.

'What's the matter with her? Why can't she walk on her own?'

'She's very uncooperative.' Mamie was half carried, half dragged into the consulting room. She stank of paraldehyde. No wonder she was uncooperative. She was drugged out of her mind. With difficulty we completed the rest of the tests but she was beyond holding a rational conversation.

'Why has she been given paraldehyde?' I asked.

'She flew into a rage because Doctor Brown would not let her have her letter, so she had to be punished.'

'What do you mean, punished?'

'Put in like a padded cell on her own till she come to her senses but she didn't, just went on creating whenever anyone came near her, demanding her letter so we had to drug her to calm her down.'

I felt a hollow feeling of responsibility. It was surely MY letter that had been the cause of the trouble. I had found out that Mamie could read simple words and had sent her a letter saying I would call for her on Sunday and take her out to tea with my family. I knew I would have to clear this with the Medical Superintendent but in my naivety had not anticipated any difficulty. It was a cardinal error and one poor Mamie paid for dearly.

Later that afternoon I received a telephone call from Dr Brown's secretary. In effect I was summoned to Lennox Castle although technically I was invited to 'take tea' with him. I could easily have refused but I was not only curious to see the place but also concerned about the conditions inside and welcomed the opportunity to meet him.

I enjoyed the drive out of the city to the foothills of the Campsie hills before turning into the extensive grounds round the Victorian Gothic mansion which formed the hub of the hospital and the domestic offices of the medical superintendent. Once admitted to the drawing room I met the man himself. We shook hands and he invited me to be seated in a low chair beside a small table set for afternoon tea in front of a coal fire. To my astonishment a maid wearing a beribboned cap and apron brought in the teapot and hot water. I had not seen such a phenomenon since the pre-war days of genteel Wonersh.

Unhappily, that was the end of my entertainment. I was subjected to a vitriolic diatribe in which I was accused of undermining his authority, abetting disobedience and causing distress to HIS patient. I should know that all letters to patients were vetted by him and were withheld if they would cause difficulties. It was unfortunate that, due to an oversight Mamie had been told that she had had a letter from me. She was a very difficult and violent patient who would need much discipline and training before she could be allowed out into the world.

I was amazed at his anger. It was almost palpable and it was obviously impossible to hold any kind of rational discussion with him. I rose to my feet with some difficulty, as the chair was low.

'I think there is little point in my staying longer. I disagree with almost everything you say. My motive for asking the child to tea was purely that of kindness for a poor unfortunate human being who has had more than her fair share of misery.' Mamie did not return for her third set of tests and we were told she had escaped over the wall into the public road with all her worldly goods in a plastic bag. She was never traced.

My next sidelight into the workings of the hospital came through the Domiciliary Service. I was visiting a patient of very limited intelligence. I knew she had had a child who had been taken into care and that she was now married to the father of the baby. The couple were trying to persuade the social services to allow the little girl to live at home with them. I chapped the door which was opened by a very short young woman carrying a small case in her hand. She took me into a dimly lit room with the curtains safety pinned shut and a single 40 watt bulb in the bare overhead socket. Lizzie was lying in bed, not ill, she normally only got up about one o'clock. The stale air was heavy with cigarette smoke, unwashed bodies and soiled clothes. I sat on the bed and the wee lady perched on a chair. Between them I managed to unravel the story.

'We was both in Lennox Castle, ken. Then we was sent to an old people's home run by the Sally Ann (Salvation Army). We lived in and worked as maids. They were quite strict but it was better than that old Castle and we were able to slip out to the dancing.' They both started giggling.

I hardly needed to ask, 'What happened then?'

'Well, Lizzie fell (became pregnant) and when the Major (Salvation Army Officer in charge of the home) found out, we was both sent back.'

'We had to go to the Medical Superintendent,' said Lizzie. 'He wanted to know all about it.'

'What sort of 'all about it'?' I asked.

'Well, did I have my knickers off and did we do it standing up and things like that.'

Marion interjected, 'To tell you the truth Dr Wilson, it was not so much of an interview, it was more of an intercourse.'

Out of the mouths of babes and sucklings I thought. Marion could not read or write although she offered to type my letters on the child's portable typewriter she always carried with her. She did not even realise that the resulting gibberish could not be read but she had some insight into the workings of human nature.

Lizzie had been sent to the maternity unit at Stobhill Hospital to have her baby and was thought to be incapable of looking after the child herself. She was allowed to leave Lennox Castle and was given a Corporation flat and then married the baby's father. As long as there was a possibility that she might be allowed to have little Senga home she was willing to use family planning but when the decision was made that the child should stay in care, I knew she would want another baby. Sure enough she wanted her coil out.

'What does Tom say?'

'Och, it's nuthin tae dae wi' him.'

'Oh, come on Lizzie, he is your man,' I expostulated.

'Mebbe aye and mebbe no,' she replied enigmatically.

'What do you mean?'

'Well Ah've got this boyfriend in the next street – he cuts thru the close, ken, when Tom's awa tae the broo(unemployment exchange) an last time he mounted me he said he'd reelly like a babby.'

I did not feel it was appropriate to enter into a discussion on paternity rights and she was adamant that the IUD must be removed. I took it out without difficulty and three months later she was pregnant. This time the combined efforts of the NHS and the Social Work Department were laid on to help her keep the baby. She stayed in the maternity unit for ten days while she was helped to learn how to look after the child and then went home by taxi, a midwife escorting her. She had daily visits from a health visitor and a social worker as she was now living on her own, Tom having walked out and her 'boyfriend' keeping a very low profile. She flatly refused to use towelling diapers and demanded, and got, disposable nappies. These were relatively new and very expensive at that time. I had much sympathy with her point of view having had to cope with washing and drying terry towelling squares for all of my six children but I had had a washing machine and hot water. She may have had a low IQ but she had a natural cunning which she used to take advantage of every possibility. She left Stobhill two weeks before Christmas and on the festive day pushed Angela in the donated buggy up to the Maternity Unit. She was welcomed back by the staff who had got to know her well both as an out- and in-patient. She enjoyed her Christmas dinner on the ward and presents for mother and baby from the tree. Then laden with supplies of baby milk, nappies, and two boxes of chocolates she, the baby and the buggy were helped into a taxi courtesy of a generous midwife.

After two years of sustained effort on the part of the authorities it was decided that Angela would have to be removed from Lizzie's care. By this time she was, in reality, a prostitute working from home and was known throughout the neighbourhood as being available to any man with five pounds to spare. It was not this, so much as her inability to look after the little girl, especially when she started walking, that caused concern. Lizzie appeared to have no concept of danger as far as the child was concerned. Angie wandered unchecked on the street, played on the unguarded hearth and was fed baked beans and Irn Bru (the Glasgow equivalent of

Coke). Her mother was not unduly upset about her removal and about a year later asked if I could arrange for her to be sterilised as 'Ah dinnae want tae gang thru' all that hassle again.' I was only too delighted to oblige as I was aware that her lifestyle increased the likelihood of pelvic infection with her IUD which she had willingly had fitted after Angela was born.

Several years later I came across her in an Adult Training Centre. She greeted me like a long-lost sister, giving me a hug and asking me to admire a bead necklace she was making. She was a regular and enthusiastic daily attender. The routine of games, music and occupation had changed her life and very much for the better. She took pride in her appearance, had her hair done every week in the centre and joined in the sing-songs and dancing. She was still a little unpredictable and nobody asked what she did in the evenings. It was good to see her taking such a positive hold on her life.

In the course of time there were changes in the medical and administrative management at Lennox Castle and I was asked if I would visit on a regular basis to give contraceptive advice to some of the women patients. Attitudes were changing from custodial care to integration in the wide world outside. Initially the aim was ostensibly to prevent unwanted pregnancies within the hospital environment as the strict segregation of the sexes, unless directly supervised, was being relaxed. Even sitting side by side on a garden wall or, worse still, holding hands, had been punished. Unhappily although most of the medical staff were behind the liberalising of the regime, some of the older nursing staff were totally against it.

The higher grade female patients occupied 'The Huts'. Many of these women should never have been in a mental deficiency institution at all and were there largely for social reasons. Two had had babies in their mid-teens, who had, of course, been taken from their young mothers and been 'put up' for adoption. Several were in regular contact with their families but I usually had no idea of the circumstances that had brought them to this hospital in the first place.

'The Huts' were exactly that – four long single storey buildings that looked as though they should have been pulled down years before. The nurse in charge of one of these huts was almost as wide as she was tall and had a fearsome number of black hairs sprouting from her chin, and a noticeable moustache. She was totally against my activities and told me in unvarnished words, 'It's against my religion to go against the laws of nature by using any artificial form of birth control.'

She went on to tell me, 'In my opinion it's downright disgusting even to think of these poor mentally deficient girls being allowed to have a relationship which should only happen in the marriage bed.'

The space in each hut was so restricted that during the day all the beds had to be pushed together towards the far end of the ward. This left enough room near the old iron stove in the middle of the floor to allow each woman to have a chair not too far from the only source of heat. The ward sister had one of the two small rooms on either side of the door and she ushered me into it to hold my family planning consultations. She said the door must not be closed as she needed to hear the phone and had to come into her office to answer it. She also ensured there was no privacy by entering the room unannounced every few minutes to 'fetch something' or 'check up' on something else. It took nearly a year to improve the arrangements but eventually my clients consulted me in the Treatment Block where I had the use of adequate if old-fashioned equipment and the client's contraceptive supplies came from the hospital pharmacy and not my Dom bag.

Elsie was one of my first patients in Hut Two. She could read and write and should never have been in Lennox Castle. She had a boyfriend, Jim who was also a patient. They had been punished for holding hands while sitting on a wall outside the Occupational Block. Sometimes Elsie went home for a weekend to her parents' council flat in the newly built Gorbals. They had asked if Jim could go home with her to meet her parents. Elsie's mother was very devout but she also wanted what was best for her daughter. I arranged to visit her in Queen Elizabeth Square and we had a constructive discussion about how to regulate Elsie's irregular periods by giving her the pill. I was also shown the sleeping arrangements that would be put in place when Jim came to stay. Elsie would sleep with her mother, her father would use the couch in the sitting room and Jim would have the single bed usually occupied by Elsie on her visits home. I thought these arrangements were very sensible and they continued for several months until Jim was placed in sheltered housing and found a job in the Parks Department. When Elsie joined him they were housed in a flat in a respectable estate on the site of the old barracks on Maryhill Road. He was a good worker and brought in a reasonable wage while Elsie was content to be an excellent housewife. The flat was not only clean and tidy but also cheerful with bright curtains and cushions. I continued to call on her about every three months to take her fresh supplies of the pill and see how she was getting on. At each visit I expected to hear that they had decided to stop contraception and 'try for a family'. Then she told me cheerfully, 'We're no having any weans until we're mairrit. It costs an awfy lot tae git mairrit an we've got tae save up.'

'That's a very good idea. After all you and Jim are doing so well, it's just as well to leave it for a time until you're really settled.'

The next time I called Elsie opened the door with a squirming heap of hair in her arms that transformed into a very bouncy puppy which leapt from her restraining arms as soon as the door was closed.

'Er, where did you get him?' I asked trying in vain to save my tights from disaster.

'From the PDSA,' Elsie beamed. He's had a' his jags an I'm goin tae training classes wi' him.'

'That's great Elsie, he's a lovely dog.' And I silently added to myself 'how sensible for them to have opted for a dog rather than a baby.'

The dog grew and grew until six months later his head was up to Elsie's waist but he was well behaved and every day, whatever the weather she took him for a long walk. As she explained to me, 'Even if we wanted a wean, which we don't, we've no time. Buster takes a terrible lot of looking after.'

Three years later they were still not married but very happy together and Buster has many years of active life before he goes to the happy hunting grounds in the sky.

Nearly all the women who consulted me while they were in Lennox Castle were placed in the community in one type of accommodation or another. I was impressed by the care taken to find the right placement for each one according to their needs and abilities. A few went to small residential units with a great deal of support and supervision but even with these moderately and severely handicapped girls progress was made towards limited independence. Alice stayed in a Church of Scotland home and after a few months was able to go on a bus to a day centre on her own. She would never be able to look after herself entirely but she enjoyed choosing her own clothes and a change of hairstyle did wonders for her appearance. Sadly she was an epileptic and she died when she inhaled her own vomit during a fit when she was enjoying a bath. I was glad she had some real happiness and fun in those last months before she died.

Some of the patients were established in 'Key Housing' – flats where two ore three people of normal ability lived with four or five others with learning difficulties. I was invited to have a meal with one of my old clients and her friends and found the experience both interesting and disturbing. There was a total taboo on any reference to differences between the able and the less able. This resulted in very obvious problems. There was a rota for cooking, cleaning and so on and on the evening of my visit, Mandy and her boyfriend had prepared the supper. We had mashed potatoes but they were not properly cooked and the attempt to beat them had resulted in a glutinous wodge containing pea and marble-sized lumps of unyielding carbohydrate. The sausages were black on one side and pink on the other and the peas came straight from the tin, unstrained onto our plates. I saluted Ted and Yvonne who LIVED here and were prepared not only to eat it but pretend to enjoy it. I also thought it was misguided and eventually not in the best interests of their fellow flatmates. Surely one of the able should be paired with one of the less able so that the latter could learn how to cook sausage and mash properly? The ethos was such that even suggesting that one person knew how to do something better than another was considered a betrayal of trust.

I suppose this was the inevitable swing of the pendulum away from the controlling despotism of Dr Brown's reign at the Castle. I hope a more satisfactory median way has now been arrived at.

A Tropical Interlude

In 1971 my husband was invited to give the first McFadzean Lecture in Hong Kong in honour of the retiring Professor of Medicine at the Medical School who was a Glasgow graduate. Our ultimate destination was Brisbane, where Graham had been appointed to be the visiting Edwin Tooth Professor for four weeks. In addition to Hong Kong, we were taking the opportunity to call in on several other interesting places on our route to and from Australia.

He was also a trustee of the Nuffield Foundation, in those days a wealthy charity, founded by the creator of the Austin-Morris car business, which was dedicated to promoting activities in the fields of health and education. One of its projects was concerned with teaching numeracy to children in New Guinea. Most of the people, especially in the interior, were not only illiterate but also innumerate; their way of life, with virtually no contact with the outside world until their invasion by the Japanese, had not required them to count above ten. A primary school in Lae, on the North coast, was the site of the pilot scheme. We landed in the steamy heat of Port Moresby and while Graham went off with Professor

Roy Scragg to be shown something of the embryo Medical School started by the Australians two years before, I was shown the family planning services.

The rather plump tightly encased English nurse asked me to give a talk to the trainee nurses. She drove me round in her small saloon, the dashboard and the rear window ledge embellished with strips of once white nylon fur. The nurses were mostly of Polynesian stock, the predominant ethnic group round the coast. I remember emphasising the commonality of womanhood all over the world, especially the poorly educated. Women in Glasgow were afraid of things being put inside their bodies (IUDs), were not good at remembering to take a pill every night, were afraid of their husbands' anger and disliked clinics and did not like messing about with caps and creams and the lack of convenient washing facilities made this understandable. I suggested that the women in the slums of Port Moresby were probably very similar. The audience asked many questions and seemed to appreciate my talk but I soon realised that I had committed a major error as far as the Sister Tutor was concerned. She had been trained some ten years before somewhere in the UK where the focus was on rubber goods. She was lecturing to the class about diaphragms and spermicides and her main preoccupation was how to stop the rubber from rotting in the hot humidity of the tropical climate.

The next day we flew to Goroka in the New Guinea Highlands. There was no road in those days, but the town was far from primitive and contained many substantial buildings and modern shops. It seemed as though every Christian sect from Australia to the USA was competing to exploit this so far untapped source of souls. From the Catholic Church to the Salvation Army with Seventh Day Adventists, Primitive Baptists, and Uncle-Tom-Cobley-and-All in between, there were schools, training colleges and agricultural establishments to tempt the local inhabitants to the higher ways of the West. The sight of a man riding a bicycle down the main street naked, except for a minimal tuft of grass fore and aft, brought a smile to my face. He epitomised the contrast between the two cultures and hopefully was enjoying the best practices of both.

We stayed with Dr Peter Pharoah, employed by the Institute of Human Biology, who was working at the local government hospital (Australian funded). We arrived slightly early and Graham was taken off to hear about Peter's exciting work giving injections of iodised oil to the teenage girls to prevent their babies from being born grossly handicapped (cretins) due to the iodine deficient water. Their two children were left to entertain me while Mrs Pharoah finished her preparations for the evening meal. There had recently been a very big a gathering of many of the hill tribes for dancing and feasting. There are over 600 different languages in New Guinea which gives some indication of the number of tribes, each isolated in its own inaccessible valley with little contact except that of bloody border skirmishes. The children had watched the tribal dancing, the facing lines of near naked men or women stamping the ground and waving their arms to a compulsive beat which the children demonstrated in the living room of the bungalow.

Then Paul, an articulate child of eight, went on to tell me amid fits of giggles from him and his sister, how one particular lady, wearing only a grass skirt and that most prized symbol of civilisation, a bra, had had difficulty retaining her skinny but very pendulous breast inside the garment, which of course had not been made for her. As she danced first one breast would escape and have to be fielded by her other hand and thrust back into its proper place and then the other would fall out and the process had to be repeated. The children were in the middle of a graphic re-enactment of this hilarious scene when their mother's scandalised face appeared in the doorway and cut it short. I was glad she did not arrive earlier and deprive me of an unforgettable vignette of Goroka in transition.

We had half a day to spare before we flew over the mountains in a four-seater plane to Lae. Graham asked Peter if there were still surviving cases of Kuru that we could visit. When the Japanese were finally expelled from New Guinea, the Australians had discovered this hitherto unknown disease. It affected women and children almost exclusively. They became increasingly paralysed and finally were afflicted with uncontrollable writhing movements, especially of the face, before they inevitably died. The local name 'Kuru' meant laughing sickness and referred to their facial contortions. The discovery caused great excitement in the medical world and a fiercely competitive race began between the Australians and the Americans to find the cause, which the latter eventually won. At first it was thought to be genetic, because it was confined to only two tribes and predominated in women. The other theory concentrated on their diet and hundreds of specimens were analysed for toxins with no result. Finally the horrid truth began to emerge as the scientists became more familiar with local customs.

New Guinea is remarkable for having no native mammals of any size. Pigs had been introduced but were kept to be eaten only on important feasts, otherwise the diet was vegetarian. In these circumstances it is not surprising that the only common source of first class protein should not be wasted and cannibalism was the usual way of disposing of the dead. The men, as befitted warriors, took the muscle tissue and the women and children ate the offal, including the brain and nerve tissue. Research into the link between new variant Creuzfeldt-Jacob Disease and mad cows has revealed the causative agent as the deadly prion which can survive in its new host for years before the victim succumbs. Kuru belongs to the same group of progressive degenerative diseases of the nervous system. In those days it was thought to be due to a 'slow virus'. Scrapie in sheep was almost the only known example of a similar infection. The idea of human to human transmission in the food was shocking but proved to be correct. This had been elucidated several years before we visited New Guinea. The Australians had forbidden cannibalism before the discovery of the origin of Kuru but the disease had a very variable course and sometimes a long incubation period, so we were lucky. There were two cases among the North Fore tribe not far away and relatively accessible by road.

The village was on the flattened top of a small hill, surrounded by a thorn perimeter fence. Inside were half a dozen circular thatched huts. I immediately noticed a washing line stretched between two of them on which were suspended several brassieres in various colours and sizes, confirming young Master Pharoah's observations about their status value. Inside the huts low platforms were built round a central hearth which made the atmosphere in them very smoky. Basically the croft houses in use in the Scottish Highlands up to fifty years ago, were built to a similar pattern, using stone instead of wood. The only unexpected items were numerous wire coat hangers hooked onto the walls inside, collected by the young men who sometimes worked in hotels on the coast.

The patients were both women, probably in their early forties but they had little conception of age. One said she could remember hearing of the German missionaries (who had been established in a few places on the northern coast before the war). They sat on clean army blankets on the ground, one supporting herself on her hyper-extended arm. She could not walk and the other woman needed substantial support. They were looked after by three nubile girls, naked except for grass skirts, (the brassieres were obviously kept for special occasions), who kept the patients in the shade by moving a huge palm leaf round as the sun crossed the sky. They fed them and helped them to the village latrine, housed in a little hut cantilevered out over the edge of the drop. As examples of community care they could teach us a thing or two.

As for cannibalism, there was an item in the Port Moresby *Gazette* on the day we arrived – 'Judge Frees Three Who Ate Villager'. At that time Australia still had the ultimate judicial authority. Three men had been found guilty of eating the victim of a fight, but they had appealed. The Queensland judge had decided that, as this had been the customary method of disposing of the dead in the past, they should not be imprisoned for it, but were warned not to repeat the offence. What a sensible man!

Just a Little Jag

My contact with the family planning services in Hong Kong had long term consequences for the work in Glasgow. The senior doctor in the main family planning centre was an Englishwoman, Gladys Dodds, who had retired from gynaecological practice in the UK and was living permanently on the island with her sister. She was thin, grey-haired and with the educated voice one expected from her appearance. The staff liked and respected her and she ran a first rate service. Many of the medical staff, mostly women, were from mainland China who did not have western qualifications but they were hard-working and conscientious and Miss Dodds had no difficulties working with them.

I was excited to learn that she had been using an injectable form of contraception which I had read a lot about. It was a long-acting progestogen and had had extensive field trials in Thailand under the auspices of the World Health Organisation (WHO). She had started a thousand women on three monthly injections and most of these had already used the drug for from one to two years. Their medical notes were meticulously kept, the patient's weights, blood pressures, bleeding patterns and any possible side-effects being carefully recorded.

I asked her what she really thought of this new contraceptive method.

'I think it is a real breakthrough. Apart from irregular bleeding patterns that nearly always end in amenorrhoea (no periods), we have hardly any problems and no serious side-effects. Some do gain weight but as that is associated with affluence here that is almost a bonus! Of course the Chinese do love injections, but it's a great relief to most of them that they don't have to remember a pill every night.'

She asked me back to her flat to meet her sister. It was in one of those amazing skyscrapers built on an area no bigger than a tennis court but housing hundreds of people. I shamelessly picked her brains about Depo-Provera and resolved to try and introduce it to the women of Glasgow, especially the domiciliary patients.

At that time Depo-Provera was only licensed in the UK for treating ovarian cancer. The doses were enormous and most of the patients died of their disease anyway. Little was known about its long-term use in very much smaller doses as a contraceptive, apart from the material published by WHO. When I returned to Glasgow after three months absence (how lucky I was, it would never be allowed today), I went to see both Professors of Obstetrics and Gynaecology in their separate offices. Ian Donald at the Western Infirmary was unexpectedly supportive. He genuinely believed in effective contraception as he loathed abortion. He was a devout High Anglican and a good friend but he knew my liberal views on termination of pregnancy and, in spite of his support over Depo-Provera, he consistently blocked the establishment of a family planning clinic in the Queen Mother's Maternity Hospital.

Malcolm MacNaughton at the Royal Infirmary was a very different man. Just as true a Christian but with a deep humanity which had been nurtured by the doyen of gynaecology in Scotland, Sir Dougal Baird in Aberdeen, he was eager to alleviate the problems of women living in dire poverty in the East End of the city. He knew that social circumstances had as much to do with the higher than average number of deaths related to child birth, as to poor medical care. When he arrived in Glasgow in 1968 women attending for their first antenatal visit at Rotten Row (the Royal Maternity Hospital) were, on average, already 28 weeks pregnant. He changed the whole ethos of antenatal care. If women did not come to the hospital, the hospital should go to them. This was a revolutionary idea at the time. Antenatal clinics were started in grim housing schemes like Easterhouse, five miles from the city centre where the hospital was located. The atmosphere was user-friendly and welcoming and gradually women began to attend earlier and the peri-natal mortality rates to fall.

Professor MacNaughton immediately realised the potential of Depo-Provera. Staff in his department were delivering hundreds of women every year who had four or more children, many with more than ten. The hazards of pregnancy for both mother and child increase with each confinement. Grand multipara (women with more than six pregnancies) were the rule rather than the exception at Rotten Row in 1971. He offered to supply me with the drug from the hospital pharmacy where a supply was kept to treat cancer. It was dispensed in a small vial with a rubber cap so that a needle could be inserted and the correct dose aspirated by syringe. The vials had been standing a long time on the shelf and the contents had separated into a thick white sediment and a clear supernatant fluid. It took several minutes of vigorous shaking to mix the two properly. It was not until the drug was licensed for short-term use as a contraceptive that we were able to order it in single dose vials through the city pharmacy along with all the other contraceptive supplies.

Over the next ten years we used it increasingly for domiciliary patients and, gradually, as doctors became more familiar and confident about prescribing it, we offered it to women at all the clinics in Glasgow. I lectured about it on many family planning courses and its use especially among the disadvantaged, became widespread throughout the UK, but only in clinics. General practitioners remained wary of it until it received official blessing.

In addition to the obvious advantage of only being required to be administered every three months, the method was particularly suitable for women who did not want their partners to know that they were practising contraception. A packet of pills was easily found and, if the man knew he was going to serve a prison sentence, he did his worst to make sure she was pregnant before he went inside. The pills were burnt (open fires were the norm then) and even intra-uterine devices were not secure. The men usually detected their presence as the threads protruded through the cervix so we advised women to tell their partners that they had had one fitted. One gentleman was so determined to ensure his wife's fidelity that using the inside of a toilet roll as a speculum, he removed the device with his wife's eyebrow tweezers. Depo-Provera could not be removed and the injection into the upper and outer quadrant of the buttock ensured that it was not detected. It was the only form of family planning over which the woman had complete control.

For many it resulted in their periods stopping completely, especially as the number of injections increased. It was very important to warn the prospective user that this was likely to happen as the myths surrounding menstruation were part of women's cultural background. Periods, 'the curse', 'the time in the month', 'ma illness', indicate the general view that menstruation was an affliction women had to bear and the proscriptions on intercourse in Judaism, Islam and, until recently, Christianity, reinforce the belief that women are unclean and men must protect themselves from the 'bad blood' which is shed during that time. If the blood is bad it must obviously be got rid of, otherwise it will poison the body and cause all manner of unpleasant consequences. These beliefs were held as strongly in West Africa as they were in the deprived populations of Glasgow. Most young women would accept the idea that 'the jag' acted in a similar way to lactation, which also inhibits ovulation and stops menstruation. Few in Glasgow knew this from direct observation as breast feeding was almost unknown among our Dom patients but most accepted it as a fact.

No period pains, no premenstrual tension, no cost of sanitary protection and almost one hundred per cent protection from pregnancy were benefits that far outweighed the slight discomfort of an injection for most, but there were a few who needed a lot of persuasion. One group were the elderly mothers of mentally handicapped girls who were constantly worried by the concept of the 'bad blood'. 'Where did it go?'

I was asked to visit a severely handicapped 14 year old who was supposed to be attending a special school. She had been barred because of her unpredictable anti-social behaviour. A bus had collected her each day to take her to school but when she was menstruating she removed her sanitary towel and wrapped it round the drivers neck on more than one occasion. It was hoped that if she had the injection her periods would stop and this particular problem would be solved.

I was asked into the living room where the girl sat crosslegged in a corner of the settee, rocking herself backwards and forwards while she crooned repetitively. A large Alsatian occupied most of the hearth rug. I sat in one of the armchairs on either side of the fire with Mrs Downie opposite. She was short and round and in her early sixties and had outlived three husbands. She was 48 when Pat was born and she could just read the headlines in the *Daily Record*. She agreed eventually to Pat having the jag, mainly because hygiene was a problem at 'that time in the month' but she sensibly asked for it to be tried once and then we would talk about it again when the next one was due. Pat had not been to school for over six months but her mother was unconcerned by this and obviously was happy to have her daughter with her. I was concerned about the child's education and got in touch with the appropriate authorities to find she had somehow slipped through the net, no doubt with total lack of cooperation from her mother. In due course a school inspector called on the Downies to assess their situation. Being afraid of an attack by the Alsatian he opted to sit on the settee and was promptly bitten by the child who was sitting next to him. It transpired later that biting was the other antisocial habit that had led to her removal from school. Mrs Downie won in the end through sheer inertia. She managed to spin the official procedures out until her daughter was sixteen and was no longer required to attend school. Long before she reached that age her mother had become concerned about the whereabouts of the bad blood and decided that Pat should have no more DP. As she never went out except with her mother and corporation bus drivers are better protected from their passengers than the school bus drivers used to be, there was no need for me to continue my visits.

I have given injections of Depo-Provera in many unlikely situations; once by the light of a street lamp, inside my mini. Jube was the youngest of three sisters who earned their living on the streets. She was only fifteen and she believed her mother was unaware that she was following in her siblings' footsteps. I had left messages for her to meet me but she had not turned up and her next 'jag' was due. I called at the house in Tambowie Street in Temple, an unexpected island of deprivation in the midst of working class respectability in those days. Her two older sisters welcomed me and I dispensed whatever contraceptives were appropriate but I had to find an excuse to see Jube on her own. One of the other girls complained of 'an itch down below'.

'I've got just the right cream for that down in the car. Perhaps Jube here could come down with me and save me coming back up the stairs?'

She agreed with alacrity, got into the passenger seat and I duly gave the injection into her thigh before she jumped out, tube of Canestan (for treating her sister's itch) in hand.

In the early days there was still a 'Steamie' in Springburn – a public wash house where women took their laundry to scrub the sheets and the overalls in deep sinks and squeeze them through huge mangles before taking 'the washing' home in an old pram to hang it out on the back green. I had been given the address of this particular woman who had recently had her tenth child, but had had some difficulty finding it. The condemned tenement was in a short cul-de-sac, whose name in the street guide was indecipherably at the junction of two pages. I found it at last but my difficulties were not over. 'Ground Right' I had been informed but the close had already lost half its floor boards and I had to walk sideways to reach the door. Once there a small child told me that her Maw was at the Steamie. Fortunately this was at the end of the same street and, on going inside, I soon located Mrs Kenny.

I am very glad I had this experience of seeing inside one of these traditional Glasgow establishments. Before many years had passed they had all gone, no longer needed in the era of washing machines. There was a great sense of camaraderie amid the noise and the steam but both these factors also made it possible to find a little privacy among the piles of wet clothes and steaming sinks. Mrs Kenny did not want her husband to know that she was not prepared to have yet another pregnancy and the jag suited her admirably. As her lord and master was slumped on the sofa at home sleeping off the effects of the booze from the night before, she asked if I could give it her there and then, which I was pleased to do.

One night, not long after my husband had eventually come home after three months in hospital and we had gone to bed early, the phone rang.

'Hallo, who is it?' My immediate thought was that something had happened to one of the family. It was 10.15, too late for a social call.

'It's Father Jacinelli from St Philomena's in Blackhill. I want to know what business you have in using my parishioners as guinea pigs.'

'I'm sorry, I've no idea what you are talking about and it is rather late. . .'

'Giving experimental injections paid for by a drug company to these vulnerable women,' he interrupted me fiercely.

'Father, it's not like that.' Eventually I calmed him down enough to agree that I should meet him the next day over a cup of coffee at his priest's house.

I duly presented myself and was invited to join him in the parlour. He was a well-built imposing-looking man in middle age who sternly demanded to know what I was doing to his flock. I explained that far from using his parishioners as experimental fodder to obtain results that could be used to promote this new contraceptive in the third world as he had suggested, I had seen it used in the Far East and wanted my patients in Glasgow to benefit from it. I told him I had the support of both professors of obstetrics and that Depo-Provera had been used on a large scale by the World Health Organisation for many years. We discussed the matter further and then our talk turned to other things and he discovered that I had come from Sheffield in the late 1960s.

'My sister is a biochemist and works in the Jessop Hospital for Women,' he said. 'I don't suppose you ever came across her?'

It so happened that I had. Indeed I had been intimately involved in the research she was doing into certain hormone levels in pregnancy. This had entailed collecting every drop of urine from the time the pregnancy was diagnosed until four weeks after delivery. For eight months I had peed by means of a plastic funnel into a large plastic bottle. Each 24-hour collection had to be delivered to the Jessop daily. I had had to take my apparatus with me to dinner parties and excursions as well as to work. My bladder capacity, especially during pregnancy, was somewhat limited.

Obviously the frosty relationship between the good Father and myself had thawed considerably by the time I felt free to explain these biological details to him.

Finally he as said as I left, 'I cannot agree with what you are doing but I respect your motives for doing it,' and he gave me his blessing.

Depo-Provera had been given a licence for short term use as a contraceptive in 1972, to protect the wives of men who were having vasectomies and as an interim measure while the woman waited for the three months considered advisable after delivery, before they were sterilised themselves. We had been using it without limit of time since 1972 without major problems. The manufacturers, Upjohn, applied for a licence for long term use in 1982. The data had to be presented to the Committee on the Safety of Medicines (CSM) for approval and the Department of Health then granted the licence. The enquiry was very thorough and a great deal of material was demanded and provided over a period of many months. Finally the CSM recommended approval with a few warnings in the small print. To our total amazement and disgust the Department of Health refused to issue the licence. This was the first time **ever** that a recommendation from the CSM had not been followed. The Minister of Health had only been in post one day. This was a political decision made by civil servants who knew nothing of the medical or social benefits of this method of contraception but who were swayed, as always, by adverse media publicity that emanated from the USA. It was a re-run of the Dalkon Shield story, a mishmash of distorted science, scare stories and accusations of racial abuse. A much publicised version of a pseudo-scientific paper purported to prove that it caused cancer, resulted in permanent infertility and caused birth defects. It was also said that white male doctors were forcing black women in Haarlem to have the injection against their will.

There was no truth in any of these statements but they were taken up by the leftwing press over here and the result was that the lily-livered permanent civil servants in the Ministry of Health bowed to the clamour of the uninformed mob. This did not affect our use of Depo because we had been using it for a decade without a licence. We had more experience than any other doctors in the UK and were confident that WHO and the CSM were not wrong in endorsing its use.

Under the terms of the Medicines Act 1968 a company that had had a licence refused, was allowed to appeal. This had never happened before and there was considerable delay in setting up the Special Committee to hear the appeal. It finally took place over three days, more than a year later. It was down to Upjohn to prove its case. I gave evidence at some length as did some of my family planning colleagues who were also familiar with its clinical use, but much of the evidence was pharmacological and biochemical. Truth prevailed in the end and Depo-Provera was fully licensed in 1984.

Abortion

The Abortion Act became law in 1967 and doctors working in family planning clinics quickly realised that patients presenting with requests for termination of pregnancy were going to form a significant part of their caseload. A few did not want to be involved but most of us believed that abortion should be part of the sevices offered by family planning clinics. In Glasgow we played a larger role than in most other parts of the UK as not only were nearly half the population Roman Catholic but a substantial number of general practitioners were too. The Act requires the signature of two independent medical practitioners on the certificate authorising the termination of the pregnancy. One is that of the referring doctor and the other that of the gynaecologist who has agreed to carry out the procedure.

From the start there were gross inequities in the working of the Act. In the 1980s in England less than half the abortions were carried out within the NHS but in Scotland the figure was over 90% This overall percentage concealed a great disparity both between and within Health Boards. Glasgow was divided into five districts each of which contained at least one hospital or gynaecology unit equipped to undertake terminations but the chances of a woman being successful in obtaining one depended on where she lived. This geographical lottery was further complicated by different views held by various consultants regarding the validity of the grounds on which the request was made. It was essential to refer the woman to a named gynaecologist who was known to be sympathetic. This often involved personal contact, usually by phone. How I loathed having to call my friends and twist their arms in order to ensure that some particularly needy woman would have the procedure which was hers by right. Not infrequently this meant asking consultants outside Glasgow for help, especially when the pregnancy was of more than twelve weeks duration, and/or she lived in the catchment area of the Western Infirmary or the Southern General Hospital.

In the early 1970s I submitted a report on the working of the Abortion Act as I had experienced it in Glasgow. I had successfully referred over 50 women in the preceding six months, nearly half from the Glasgow Advisory Centre for the young and unmarried that had succeeded the Brook Clinic established in 1968. Once I had decided that there were valid grounds for the request I did all I could to ensure that a termination was carried out.

Occasionally the reasons given were, in my opinion, frivolous and then I gave the woman the address of private facilities in Birmingham or London. One twenty-one year old, engaged to the father of the child, said she did not want to go on holiday with a bulge above her bikini. I thought if she could afford to fly to Ibiza, she could afford to pay for her bikini line.

Two of the grounds for a request were rarely used – that the continuance of the pregnancy would risk the life of the mother and that there was a substantial risk that the child would be born with a serious mental or physical handicap. The third indication was that the continuation of the pregnancy would involve risk or injury to the mental or physical health of existing children. This enabled mothers to be referred whether they had one child or ten providing they felt they could not cope with another one. It was very rarely the mothers of ten who sought abortion, unless they had a serious medical problem. Once you have a large family, having another mouth to feed is no big deal. Your only income comes from the state (with a little help from the black economy) and your concern is for today and possible tomorrow but not next week or next year. The most usual clause invoked was 'that the continuation of the pregnancy would be a greater risk to the health of the mother than if it was terminated', as, statistically, the risk of death from pregnancy was greater than the risk from an abortion.

Mrs Sweeney sent me a message at the Blackhill clinic. 'Would I pop in to see her sometime that morning?' She lived across the road from the clinic but had six children under eight and found it difficult to leave her house, a four apartment ground floor flat in Acrehill Street. I walked over the road and knocked on the door. No answer. I lifted the flap of the letter box.

'Hallo, is that you Mrs Sweeney?'

I could see into the living room through the slit but all I could see was the usual tumble of toddlers and small children on the bare boards. The family were prize examples of the 'bare bottoms on bare boards' syndrome. The baby who could not yet walk wore a nappy (so that he would not pick up any splinters as he shuffled about) but nothing on top, while his siblings wore T-shirts or vests but no pants. This did not mean they were house-trained. It was just easier for them to wet the floor and anything more solid was wiped up with newspaper and put in the bin (usually).

'It's Dr Wilson, you asked me to call.'

As I watched, the door of the broom cupboard was pushed open and the lady of the house emerged with some difficulty, knocking over a bucket in the process.

'Ah'll no be a minute,' she called. I lowered the flap and waited. The door opened and a rather red-faced Mrs Sweeney let me in.

'What was all that about?' I asked.

'Ah thocht ye was the priest.'

'But why were you hiding from him?'

'Yon Father Jacinelli knows all that goes on in the scheme.'

'So what, you have'nt done anything wrong?' I queried.

'Naw, no yet, but Ah'm thinking on it.'

She told me she had 'fallen' again and felt she 'couldnae cope' with any more weans and wanted the pregnancy terminated. I sat down and explained to her what this entailed. She wanted to be sure she was asleep when it was done. As all abortions were done under general anaesthesia at that time I had no difficulty in reassuring her. But I was far from convinced that this was what she really wanted. She was no church-goer but Theresa, her eldest, was shortly to take her First Communion.

'You talk it over with your man, and I'll come back next week.'

The following Tuesday I chapped her door again and this time there was no delay in her answering it.

'Ah've changed ma mind. Ah'll just have the wean.' I was not surprised.

'Did Father Jacinelli find out or was it your man?'

'Nah, it wasnae onything like that. Ah havenae tellt him. You said Ah would have to stay in hospital for the night?'

'Yes, that's right. You can't go home after you've had an anaesthetic.'

'Ah cannae staun hospitals. Ah'll jist go through wi' it. Ye tellt me Ah'd hivtae gang in next week, ken, an Ah'm feart, so Ah'll bide here jist the same.'

'But you'll have to go in to have the baby,' I remonstrated.

'Oh, aye but that's no fer months and anyroad Ah'll mebbe hae the wean at hame. Ah've only got tae the hospital wance. Ah ay seem to leave it too late.'

I smiled to myself as I left. I was not surprised by her decision but, while I thought she had been struggling with her conscience (or her husband's), it was her fear of hospitals and the postponing of the evil day to the distant future, when, in the event, she might be able to deliver herself at home. **That** had been the deciding factor.

Reading now some of the case histories I included in that early report I am well aware of how much things have changed for the better but it is salutary to be reminded of how barbaric the attitudes of some consultants were to the predicaments of women referred to them for help. One ploy, used by both unsympathetic GPs and certain gynaecologists was to appear to agree to the request but to employ repeated delays so that by the time the operation should have been done it was too late. Ten of the cases I cited were of women I saw at Black Street. The V.D. clinic was part of the Royal Infirmary whose Professorial Unit had a very liberal approach but, unfortunately, someone had decreed that all gynaecological problems referred from Black Street should be seen by another consultant with a less liberal attitude.

A single mentally handicapped girl of 19 was brought to see me by her 34 year old Indian consort as he thought she might have a venereal disease. She had spent her seventeenth and eighteenth years in a hospital for the mentally subnormal. Her mother was in permanent care for the criminally insane after murdering the patient's two illegitimate infants. Her partner said he intended to marry her and that she was living with his relatives, but she had had a big row with him and run away to Perth (surely the most unlikely place for what followed!). She was picked up by a Nigerian who gave her gonorrhoea and made her pregnant. Mr Singh said he still intended to marry her, but not if she had an African baby.

Her period was only three days overdue when I first saw her, a pregnancy test was positive at twelve days (this was long before the instant kits available now). I referred her for the requisite psychiatric appointment (two weeks later); the request was valid and she was referred to the gynaecologist. No word at 10 weeks; intervention by me, seen at 11 weeks – admission date to be sent; 13 weeks, back to see me as still no word; finally, termination by hysterotomy at 15 weeks. Her partner cared for her enough to persist in spite of his limited knowledge of English and the baffling delays of the system.

I referred a prostitute to another hospital who lived in its catchment area. She was turned down. The consultant said, 'If we started to do those sort of women the word would get around and they would never learn to behave themselves'!

A month after this a patient was referred to me by the same gynaecologist with a request for my signature on the certificate. The GP had referred the patient but had not anticipated the consultant's agreement and refused to sign it himself! Of course I was willing to do so, once I had seen her. My opinion of the specialist was irrelevant to her problem.

In the seventies and early eighties abortion was a very hot topic and attracted a great deal of publicity. I took part in numerous debates on television and radio, student debating societies and church groups and gave many talks to the senior classes in the more enlightened schools. Usually the two sides – 'pro-life' and 'pro-choice' were fairly evenly balanced, but not always. I was asked to contribute to a half hour programme in the Scottish Television studios in Glasgow. The batting was opened by a recorded interview with Thomas Winning, by then a Cardinal, who was seconded by a mere Bishop. I had been told I would have two slots, one after the Bishop and the next after a Catholic gynaecologist, before the 'discussion' was wound up by the presenter. I said my two sentences in reply to the Bishop, holding my fire for a final broadside, only I was never allowed to deliver it. As we walked off the set I remarked in friendly but slightly ironic tone, 'Well, I was rather outnumbered wasn't I? I was the only non-Catholic on the programme.'

One of the camera men riposted, 'Oh,no, you were the only Prod in the studio, we're all Micks here'!

We did have some lighter moments investigating what our patients sometimes had to cope with when desperately seeking a termination. Malcolm MacNaughton, Professor of Gynaecology and

Obstetrics at the Royal Infirmary had been asked to investigate privately-run abortion services and he asked if I could help. Sister Grace's Clinic operated in St Enoch Square near the city centre. It was the Glasgow outreach of an agency based in Leeds. We had some reason to be dubious about its clinical standards and methods of working, One young woman had travelled to Leeds for the termination of her supposed pregnancy, only to be told when she got there, that there had been a mistake in the urine test and she was not pregnant at all. Another had had an abortion in Leeds but came to us because she still had morning sickness. She was at least 14 weeks pregnant and it was very difficult to arrange a termination at so late a stage. A third patient had had an incomplete evacuation and began to bleed heavily requiring admission to hospital. We had been told also that the results of pregnancy tests were announced to the whole waiting room together with the name of the unfortunate victim.

I arranged to visit the clinic *incognito* with Sister Wallace's daughter, Linda who, at 18, was a suitable age for the deception. As my Glasgow accent is far from convincing I left Linda to do most of the talking, but I think I looked the part in an old mackintosh and head scarf. We took a urine specimen from one of our (intendedly) pregnant colleagues in an Irn Bru bottle and presented ourselves at the reception desk in the waiting room. We were asked into a small private room to give our details and we did not find that any of the stories regarding lack of privacy were borne out. The place was rather shabby but the staff did their job adequately and they did not pretend to be anything other than a referral agency. I confess we were slightly disappointed not to have uncovered a more dubious establishment but we both enjoyed this unconventional break from our usual routines.

Don't Give Me That Hoary Old Chestnut

Issues surrounding underage sex and the possible rights of parents to control the information, advice and treatment given to their children dominated contraception in the 1980s. I believe I was the precipitating cause of the entire Gillick saga which started with a private letter to me and ended in the House of Lords.

One morning early in February 1982 I was finishing off some notes at my usual Wednesday clinic at Claremont Terrace, when a nurse put her head round the door,

'You're wanted on the phone, Doctor Wilson.' I looked up. The switchboard did not normally interrupt me when I was doing a clinic.

'It's a call from London,' she added.

I went quickly to the phone in the corridor, the only one on this level.

'Hello, Dr Wilson speaking.'

'Ah, Elizabeth. This is Dr Thomas Stuttaford. Did you know you were going to be prosecuted for compounding a felony?'

'What on earth do you mean?' I had met the medical correspondent of *The Times* once but we were hardly close friends! Now here he was, giving me a friendly warning of what was about to happen.

'There has been a press release from the Catholic Press Office here stating that Archbishop Winning has submitted a deposition to Strathclyde's Chief Constable. This states that, following confirmation received from England, you have been guilty of compounding a felony.'

'But, what am I supposed to have done?' I asked.

'Prescribed condoms for boys whose girlfriends are under sixteen,' he replied.

A great light shone.

'Of course, now I know what it's all about. I had an article published in the *British Journal of Family Planning* a month or two ago concerning young people under the age of sixteen who had come to Claremont Terrace in the previous year. Some of them needed contraception and a few of the girls didn't want the pill, so I gave them condoms as an alternative.'

Nowadays we would recommend both, but this was in the pre-AIDS era. We both knew it was a crime to have intercourse with a girl under sixteen, whether she was willing or not.

'That explains it then,' he replied. 'I just thought you would like to know what was in the wind before you get plagued by reporters. I'd get on to my Defence Union straight away if I were you.'

I thanked him sincerely and did exactly that before arranging an immediate interview with my boss, the Chief Administrative Medical Officer down at the Greater Glasgow Health Board offices. Dr George Forwell was entirely supportive during the next three slightly anxious months. He contacted the Scottish Executive in Edinburgh and assured me that he would inform me of any legal developments. There was a lot of publicity. 'SEX ADVICE STORM', ARCHBISHOP SPARKS OFF POLICE INVESTIGATION', 'CHILDREN AND SEX', 'WOMAN DOCTOR GAVE BOYS CONTRACEPTIVES' shouted the *Daily Mail* and the *Evening Times*.

The 'English' source of all this mischief was Mrs Victoria Gillick, a thirty two year old mother of nine from Wisbech in Cambridge-shire. Shortly after the publication of my factual account in the BJFP I had received a four-page letter from East Anglia deploring my activities. The writer was particularly upset because the majority of the youngsters attended the clinic without their parents' knowledge, let alone their consent. She ended her epistle by saying that, 'as a Christian mother' she was very distressed to discover that doctors could behave in such an irresponsible fashion. I replied along the lines that I thought it was better for children to seek help and advice which would encourage them to behave responsibly than for a young girl to become pregnant when she was not ready for it. I rather foolishly commented that I did not see what difference being a 'Christian mother' made to the situation and that surely 'Muslim mothers' would feel the same. She wrote back almost by return in a much more hostile and aggressive manner, attacking me personally. I thought it best to ignore this second missive. There was a lack of spontaneity and an awkwardness of phrasing in this second letter which made me suspect it had been dictated by someone else and then handwritten by Victoria.

Neither the police nor the Procurator Fiscal ever contacted me. Eventually Dr Forwell told me that he had been advised that there was no case to answer, as charges must relate to specific named persons. A report in a scientific journal of five unnamed females under the age of sixteen who had been given condoms for their unknown partners to use if they decided to have intercourse, did not constitute evidence against the person who prescribed them. Male contraceptives were already freely available in many public lavatories, so the whole issue was stirred up as a means of highlighting increasingly liberal attitudes. The young were being encouraged to seek professional advice about their sex lives and the Roman Catholic Church was strongly opposed to these views. It also propelled Victoria Gillick into the limelight, a situation to which she was not averse. Before this she had been involved in a campaign to repatriate Ugandan Asians.

This was the preliminary skirmish in a war that was to last three years. It only ended with a final battle in the House of Lords which gave its decision in 1985. Victoria achieved the ultimate accolade of fame (or notoriety) as the phrase 'gillick competent' has now passed into legal jargon and the 'g' has become lower case, as a result of her much publicised legal actions.

The topic attracted media interest like wasps to jam and, as a result, those of us who had made no secret of our practical and counselling roles with underage young people, were bombarded with requests for interviews, radio discussions and occasionally TV confrontations.

There were two issues involved which were closely intertwined. It was, and is now, illegal to have intercourse with a girl under sixteen. This does not stop many youngsters from doing it. I, and colleagues like me, believe it is preferable for them to have free and easily available contraceptive advice than to run the risk of an unwanted pregnancy. Most young teenagers who want to have this type of advice, want it without the knowledge of their parents. I believe that it is often because the family relationships have broken down that they seek comfort and love outside the home and this makes it almost impossible for them to confide in a parent.

The second issue is that of confidentiality. Mrs Gillick sought to put a legal constraint on her local health authority to prevent her children from being given such advice without her agreement. Ironically, the law in Scotland was, at that time, different from that in England. To my mind it was much more sensible, as it is on a number of other issues. In Scotland, girls from the age of 12 were legally allowed to consent to their own treatment provided they knew the nature and consequences of what was proposed. Boys had to be 14. Unhappily, in my opinion, Scottish law in this matter was changed several years later to be in line with that in England, which ruled that the age of consent to treatment for both sexes was 16. The effect on clinical practice south of the border when Mrs Gillick won her appeal, was devastating. Doctors were advised that they would be endangering their careers if they prescribed for an underage girl without first obtaining parental consent. This ruling was widely publicised and it established a distrust of the medical profession among the young which took years to overcome even when, finally, the House of Lords reversed the decision.

I was eating cheeses sandwiches in an up-market hotel in Newcastle, courtesy of Tyne-Tees Television with Dr Fay Hutchinson, Senior Medical Officer of the Brook Clinics. Fay was an old friend from our student days who had been at the forefront of providing contraception for the young. It was after 11 p.m. and we were relaxing after a live confrontation with Victoria Gillick and one of her allies, a well-known medical spokeswoman for the Catholic viewpoint. This was not the first time nor the last we had been brought together by the media but I remember it because of the post script. On the screen it had all been very civilised (much to the disappointment of the producer, no doubt) but our differences were irreconcilable. Our opponents were also eating sandwiches at a nearby table. I was somewhat surprised when Victoria, wearing, as always, a bow at the back of her head, green rather than purple on this occasion, sauntered across and asked us why we persisted in poisoning young women's bodies with the chemicals in the pill. Fay replied, civilly enough, concerning the safety and efficacy of the pill.

'If only you would realise the advantages of **natural** methods, all these unnecessary deaths would be prevented,' she answered.

'We do have a special session with a rhythm trained nurse for those who want it,' I informed her. I did not explain that it was largely used by those wanting to conceive rather than those wanting to prevent pregnancy.

'Most couples want a more reliable method,' I added.

'Don't give me that hoary old chestnut about drunken husbands insisting on their rights,' she tweeted.

Unfortunately there were thousands of randy men in Glasgow, especially on Saturday nights and tens of thousands in the rest of the British Isles who insisted on satifaction, regardless of the time in the month. Victoria had already told the world that all her nine children were planned and that she was a strong supporter of breast feeding (naturally). The birth interval between children is around 18 months if the baby is breast fed for nine months so it did not take a great deal of calculation to work out that nine pregnancies in around 14 years had not required much abstinence and 'planning' hardly came into it.

It was pointless to continue a discussion with someone who was so patently out of touch with so much of the real world and Fay and I said our goodnights and went at last to bed.

The problems surrounding a pregnancy in a girl who was not yet sixteen and who did not want her parents to know about it were far from straightforward. If the pregnancy continued it was almost inevitable that it could not be concealed and most youngsters would eventually acknowledge this and tell their mothers (although sometimes there was a feminine conspiracy to delay the girl's father finding out). Occasionally an individual got away with it.

Carmen was actually seventeen and engaged to be married to a young man who was not the father of her child. Her parents were comfortably off and she had been to school at a private convent. As a wedding present her father was going to set up the young couple in their own hairdressing business. She did not come to the clinic until she was already nearly five months pregnant and in any case, abortion was totally against her principles. She wanted to be referred for maternity care without going through her family doctor who was a friend and golfing partner of her father. I arranged for her to be seen at Rotten Row after a phone call to an understanding obstetrician. I also suggested that she might like to stay in a Catholic refuge run by nuns for unmarried expectant and recently delivered mothers. She agreed to this and I contacted the Home. The nun I spoke to was barely interested in the details but wanted to be assured that the client would be able to pay the fees in advance, assuring me that if the money was not upfront,the girl would not be admitted even if she was in labour. I reiterated that she was to be admitted to the Royal Maternity Hospital when her time came. The sister was not best pleased as they had their own labour suite with a general practitioner available if a doctor was needed. These services demanded extra fees although I am sure the obstetric services at Rotten Row were much preferable for a first time young mother than the facilities offered by the convent.

In the event, Carmen stayed with a friend in the city and was duly delivered in hospital, of a healthy baby girl. She discharged herself the next day and returned in due course to sign the adoption papers. Neither her parents nor her fiancé ever found out.

Sometimes parental reaction to the knowledge of their daughter's pregnancy was not what I had anticipated. A good looking young couple presented themselves looking for a pregnancy test. The girl admitted she was only 14, although she looked more. The young man of 18, said he was her cousin and that she was staying with her uncle and aunt while her parents were on an extended cruise in the West Indies. She was indeed about seven weeks pregnant and she said she wanted an abortion. I explained that I would need the consent of a parent or guardian before I could refer her as I knew that there were virtually no gynaecologists in the area who would operate on an underage girl without parental consent. It had happened once in very exceptional circumstances, when an older sister acted as *in loco parentis* as their widowed mother was in hospital with a severe depressive illness, but in the present circumstances, it was not possible. Sandra agreed to ask her aunt to phone me on my home phone number at seven o'clock in two days time. I was not at all surprised when no call was made. I was virtually certain the young man was her sexual partner and doubted the story of the parental cruise. I was concerned about this girl who looked so mature but who was still very much a child.

It so happened that an all-day meeting was cancelled at the

last minute at the end of that week, so I had a whole afternoon free. It was a beautiful day and on an impulse I decided to visit the small Ayrshire coastal resort where Sandra said she was living. I had never been there before and had to ask my way to the address they had given.

'That's one of the schemes, it's a pretty rough area out there,' I was told. This did not deter me but as I walked back to my car I caught sight of my two lovebirds strolling away from me down the street, arms entwined and her head on his shoulder. I walked quietly up behind them.

'Hello you two. I was just looking for you.'

When they had recovered from their surprise I persuaded Sandra to give me her real address and to go home and tell her mother, then I would follow in a little while and we could discuss what was the best thing to do. This I did, knocking on the door of a substantial detached stone villa not far from the centre of the little town. A young woman answered the door carrying a toddler.

I announced myself.

'Yes, do come in. They have told me so perhaps we can go in the sitting room to talk it over.'

An attractive blonde, certainly no more than thirty she seemed remarkably un-upset.

'Are you Sandra's mum?'

'Yes, I certainly am. I had her when I was very young.'

'What do you think your husband is going to say?'

'Oh, he won't be able to say anything. We had to wait for my sixteenth birthday before we could get married!'

She assured me that there would be no problem about arranging for the termination as her GP would refer Sandra privately to 'my gynaecologist'. She did thank me for coming as she doubted whether Sandra would have told her until the pregnancy was much further advanced 'and it's so messy then, isn't it?'

I only wished that some of our other underage pregnancies could be sorted out so expeditiously.

Unlocking the Bathroom Door

From the start of my work in family planning I had been interested in the emotional and physical dynamics of the sexual act. Masters and Johnson published their *Human Sexual Response* in 1966 followed by *Human Sexual Inadequacy* in 1970, but my involvement in what we used to call 'psycho-sexual counselling' (now a very un-PC term) dated from the late fifties. Dr Elizabeth West was the senior doctor in the clinic at Attercliffe in Sheffield. She was also a Marriage Guidance Counsellor. She taught me a lot about listening and helping the client to uncover the fears and inhibitions that lay beneath their problems. In those days, analysts dominated psychiatry and their views were reflected in Marriage Guidance Council training. Asking a leading question was a cardinal sin and resulted in some ridiculous situations. Elizabeth related this story which a regional trainer told against himself.

'He was weeding his garden which was on the corner of a crossroads when a cyclist stopped and asked him the way to a nearby village.

'And which way do **you** think it is?' he responded.'

Patients attending family planning clinics realised that sex was not a taboo topic and inevitably brought their problems to the clinic staff. We felt very inadequate at first and it was not long before training seminars were set up. In London these were under the benevolent but despotic governance of Dr Tom Main who established the Institute of Psycho-sexual Medicine. The training was on analytical lines and lasted two years. Those who were considered suitable were given further training and eventually qualified as Group Leaders. Dr Main once told me that 'there were no true psychiatrists north of the Oxbridge line' so that attempts by those of us working in the field, whether in Sheffield or Glasgow, to achieve recognition by the Institute were virtually doomed from the start. We were very fortunate in Sheffield to have a superb psychatrist, Dr Lawton Tong, who was prepared to give his time freely to a small group of us who met regularly for seminars based on cases we were trying to deal with in clinical practice. Similarly in Glasgow, Dr Aston Sclare and subsequently Dr Ramon Antebbi supported and guided us with no thought of a fee.

In spite of our local efforts and the distinction of our mentors we were always beyond the Main pale. Many of the doctors who belonged to his seminars travelled distances at great personal inconvenience and expense, from Northern Ireland, Manchester and Wales for example. Most of his pupils regarded him as almost infallible and their relationship to him was like that of disciples to their guru. Criticism or a difference of opinion were heresy and not tolerated. Being too far north to be under his personal influence, it was no wonder he did not want any competition.

Fortunately one did not have to be a member of the Institute to perform a useful function in helping many people who had problems in their sex lives. By the early eighties an excellent multi-disciplinary course was set up in Edinburgh by Dr Bancroft. Zara Cent, one of our senior nurses, attended at her own expense and became the first nurse in Glasgow to be qualified. In the meanwhile we soldiered on.

'You go and get a cup of tea Mrs McNulty. Agnes and I will wait here for that solicitor woman to come back.' I was standing in the large hall of the High Court in Edinburgh holding a buff-coloured cardboard folder under my arm. Agnes McDevitt, as she had become since marriage, was a slight anxious-looking woman who appeared older than her twenty-eight years. Her mother was similarly short, plumper but also careworn and with obviously swollen ankles. She thankfully hobbled off, looking forward to taking the weight off her feet. We had already been standing there for twenty minutes.

We had been told to wait by a female solicitor of remarkably uninspiring appearance – in her forties with straggling dyed blonde hair wearing a red jacket, brown skirt and, to my amazement, red tights and shoes. We had met her as arranged half an hour beforehand. Agnes and her mother had seen her in Glasgow at the offices of probably the most well-known criminal law firm in the city, but I had never met her before. Her manner on this occasion was abrupt and casual and had already raised my hackles as she so obviously regarded her client as not worth much effort on her part. Her attitude implied that Agnes was a stupid uneducated woman who was silly enough to spend her money on a religious quibble.

She had gone to find the barrister who would be putting the case to a Judge in Chambers ie, in a private room, without the public or a jury. Agnes had never met him and did not even know his name. My impression was that our solicitor was also in the dark on this point. She had hurried off to find him and brief him concerning the facts for the first time that morning.

As we stood, searching with our eyes for her red jacket, (I suppose its conspicuousness was its one advantage) I thought about why I was here, a witness in a civil application to grant an annulment of a marriage which had lasted two years but never been consummated. I had first met Agnes and Jim at a psycho-sexual counselling session at Claremont Terrace. It was immediately evident that they were both embarrassed and nervous. Two chairs were already placed across the corner of my desk.

'Mr and Mrs McDevitt? Do sit down. What's your problem?'

Agnes looked down, clutching her hanky in her gloved hands.

'It's like this, Doctor,' Jim said. 'We've been married for a year now and, well, nothing's happened yet, if you see what I mean?'

Indeed, I did see. Non-consummation was a common problem in the west of Scotland. I had had two or three couples presenting with it in Yorkshire. It was very unusual there as far as my own experience was concerned but in Glasgow, I was seeing a new case almost every week. Looking at the couple in front of me, there was little doubt that it was not Jim's incapacity that was the root of the difficulty.

'Just tell me about it.'

'Well, she's fine as long as we've both got our clothes on and I stick to just kissing her on the face but as soon as I try to touch her below her neck, she just freezes up.'

'I can't help it. I do love him but if he puts a hand on my chest or anywhere down there, I can't stand it. It makes me feel sick,' Agnes interjected.

Hers was an extreme case but I had heard similar stories from other couples and many more where the underlying involuntary spasm of the vaginal muscles had been overcome by will power on the part of the woman or even by force on the part of the man. The resulting experience was painful and degrading for both, the vagina tight, dry and sore and the perplexed male feeling as though he had committed rape even with his partner's consent. I called this condition 'vaginal intrusion phobia' and I have yet to hear a better name.

Mrs McNulty was a very devout Catholic and had brought up her only child to be the same. Her husband had died early in Agnes's childhood. Going to Mass and Confession were part of the fabric of their lives. The old Irish parish priest had emphasised the importance of keeping oneself pure by denying fleshly desires, especially in the case of women. Even catching sight of one's naked body was a sin and touching the 'chest' or 'private parts' with the uncovered hand was encouraging carnal lust (as Adam had said, 'The woman tempted me' but she must also not tempt herself).

The wonder is that any Catholic woman brought up with these beliefs was able to enjoy a full sexual relationship whether there was a ring on her finger or not. Unhappily Agnes was still under the influence of her pint-sized but strong-minded mother and now, I feared always would be. She had not agreed to marry Jim, a kind and gentle man, until she was in her late twenties. He, poor fellow had thought her maidenly inhibitions were due to her sincere belief in keeping her virginity until after the sacrament of marriage. It had taken him many months to persuade her to seek help. I felt far from sanguine as I started to explain how, together, we would try to overcome her phobia. They were still living in Mrs McNulty's house while they both worked in pretty poorly paid jobs but were certainly eligible for a council flat.

I saw them once a fortnight over the next few months. Agnes made some progress – she could enjoy a kiss and a cuddle with only her pyjama trousers on, let Jim soap her back in the bath and could now use her hand to wash between her legs without an intervening foam sponge but the thought of herself or Jim putting anything into her vagina still made her almost physically sick. She would allow me to examine her vulva as this was for 'medical' reasons she rationalised. She would even let me put the tip of my finger in the entrance to her vagina provided I did not attempt to insert it any further. Indeed further intrusion would have been more difficult as the hymen was still intact. Jim was barred from these clinical examinations and I was not surprised when Agnes turned up alone after the first few sessions. She still hoped to surprise him one night by miraculously relaxing enough for him to 'go all the way'.

I would not undermine her primitive faith, especially while her mother's influence was ever present. I emphasised that God had enjoined mankind to be fruitful and multiply and sexual intercourse was the means he had provided. Early on I had strongly advised Jim to find somewhere else to live, as I was sure Agnes would never be able to consummate the marriage under her mother's roof. Sadly after six months of effort, Jim could take the frustration no more and he left.

A year later Agnes came back to see me as she wanted me to give evidence to support an application for the legal annulment of her marriage. She said she might want to marry again and a divorce from Jim would preclude a second marriage in a Catholic church. She wanted proof that she was still a virgin. I examined her again and, of course, found the hymen still intact. I duly recorded this in her case notes as I had on previous occasions. It was these case notes that were in the buff folder under my arm.

Mrs McNulty returned from resting her feet fortified by a cup of tea when I caught sight of the red-legged solicitor in the company of a pleasant-looking younger man wearing wig and gown. Agnes was introduced, as was her mother.

'And this is er, Doctor, er. . .'

'Wilson,' I interjected. The barrister looked surprised and raised his eyebrows interrogatively.

'I've got all her medical notes here,' I explained holding out the folder.

'Oh, I didn't realise there were written notes of the case.'

'I was consulted by Agnes and her husband about their problem over a period of several months,' I said.

'That is excellent news, and you are prepared to give evidence to that effect?'

'Of course, that's why I am here. These notes record my findings – the hymen was intact when I examined Mrs McDevitt before her husband left her.'

The lawyer interrupted, 'But that is not evidence that the marriage was not consummated before his final departure.'

'No,' I rejoined, 'but I also examined her six months after he left and she was still a virgin. Look it's all down here.'

'We must get these photocopied at once. I had no idea we had such a cast-iron case.'

He took the notes. 'I'll meet you outside the door of the court in fifteen minutes. We've just got time.' He hurried off.

I was appalled. Agnes had scrimped and saved from her meagre wages to pay the legal fees, even in those days amounting to several hundred pounds, a substantial proportion going to the useless solicitor who had not even taken the trouble to find out the facts to brief counsel. When we appeared in the courtroom the judge had a friendly exchange with the barrister. He informed all of us that this was the first time he had ever heard a case for annulment on the grounds of the wife's incapacity to complete the sexual act. He was familiar with impotent men whose wives wished to have their legal ties dissolved but this was the first time in his own experience that it was the other way round.

My verbal evidence backed up by the contemporaneous case notes won the day. The young barrister spent some time citing case law on male failures to consummate, feeling I am sure, the need to demonstrate that he had done his homework but the judge showed signs of restlessness and he cut his arguments short. The judge summed up, the annulment was granted and we all went home to Glasgow having been in court for twenty minutes.

Agnes's problem was an extreme instance of a very common attitude to sexuality and nudity which emanated from the extreme ends of the religious spectrum. Some members of both the Roman Catholic Church and the Wee Frees were united in believing that sex came from the devil!

To many women there was a taboo on any man, even their husband or a doctor, seeing their genital area. Intercourse took place in the dark, vest and pants, or in the case of the better-off, pyjamas were worn, the nether garments being slipped off under the bedclothes. The bathroom door was locked and washing below the neck was an entirely private affair. Some of this prudery was the direct result of the gross overcrowding in the old tenements when whole families lived in a 'single-end' and decency could only be maintained by the exercise of scrupulous measures to protect the susceptibilities of growing adolescents.

Geraldine Howard was an early and valued member of the Institute of Psycho-sexual Medicine. She was a remarkable and highly intelligent woman who combined elegance and good looks in a way that made her appear at least ten years younger than her chronological age. She was married to an internationally recognised paediatrician who was known to his students at Charing Cross Hospital as 'Huge Golly', a happy transposition of his real name – Hugh Jolly. They lived in a beautiful single storey house on the edge of Richmond Park surrounded by an extensive garden. This contained many mature trees planted a century before by the original owner of the estate, of which their property was only a small part. Geraldine bred budgerigars in an outside aviary. She told me that as long as a pair had a nesting site they would continue laying and rearing their chicks throughout the year. They were a delightful addition to the garden but it was the peacocks that dominated the household.

I arrived a little early one afternoon in spring and was happy to wait while Geraldine nipped down to her local shop to buy some milk. I sat on a white-painted metal chair on the terrace and observed the courting behaviour of peacocks – not so very different from humans. The male fanned out his exotic tail feathers and, vibrating with passion, advanced on his drab little lady love. She appeared to ignore him and continued to peck intermittently between the paving stones with her back to him. Just as he was about to have his wicked way, she neatly stepped under one of the garden chairs where, of course, he could not follow. This pattern was followed repeatedly, she using the patio furniture to frustrate him every time. A real prick teaser if ever there was one. He must have succeeded some times because she did lay a clutch of eggs, one a day for more than a week. The eggs had to be removed and incubated by a broody 'little brown hen'; otherwise they might have been eaten by the peahen who was not only a bad wife but an even worse mother. Geraldine, in common with other peacock breeders, knew the whereabouts of a little brown hen and had to drive post haste to the depths of Sussex to collect it. Sadly, although the hen incubated the eggs and seven fluffy chicks were hatched, they were all massacred by a fox that managed to get into their enclosure one night and the little brown hen died with them.

Hugh had written several very successful books on childcare that had been translated into many different languages. These occupied a long row on the bookshelves in the living room, each in a different coloured dust jacket. He held strong views on the benefits not only of the parents sleeping together, but also of the child sharing their bed. I thought this was a terrible idea and had spent many a cold hour kneeling by the side of a cot to soothe or comfort an unhappy child rather than bring the baby or toddler in beside us. Once in, it is very difficult to get them out and the pattern once established, is hard to break. So I thought then, and experience has only reinforced my opinion. Hugh also had strong feelings about sleeping without his wife and Geraldine hardly ever spent a night away from him. This made it difficult for her to lecture at any distance away from London. She did come to Glasgow several times but always had to fly up and down in a day and I never had the opportunity to return the hospitality she so generously gave me.

When Hugh was found to have what proved to be an incurable form of cancer, Geraldine and I became very close, as I had already lived through the stress, heartache and frustrations of a loved partner's terminal illness. Hugh made as few concessions to his disease as his physical condition allowed but this thrust a burden on his wife that she willingly bore, but only at considerable personal cost. He died after two years on the roller coaster of hope and despair that is the lot of those, patients and carers, who suffer the remissions and relapses of terminal cancer. After his death she continued to live her life to the full. She was especially delighted to have grandchildren – when I first knew her well she used to bewail the fact that her three children were all getting older and none of them had so far indicated any inclination to reproduce! Tragically she was killed in a road accident, although in uniquely Geraldine-like circumstances. She was driving a truck down the A1 preparatory to taking it loaded with supplies to Romania, which, at that time, was the current tragi-centre of Europe.

Howard was her maiden name, one of which she had reason to be proud although few of her colleagues realised that her grandfather had been the tenth Earl of Carlisle. She and her twin brother were born after their father had been killed in France in 1917. Her brother was killed as a young man early in the Second World War. No doubt these family tragedies served to strengthen the empathy she felt with those in trouble and under personal stress.

On a rather grey day not long after my husband died, I was driving towards Carlisle along the narrow road that parallels Hadrian's Wall when I saw a signpost to the left to Lanercost. The even narrower lane wound down into the valley to the rust red ruins of the Priory. Part of the old monastic buildings is still used as the parish church and, beyond the east end, the graveyard spread between the sodden fields. I knew both Geraldine's father and her brother were remembered here. After a search I found both, litchened and untended but dignified in this ancient hallowed ground.

One could learn a great deal from the appearance and demeanor of those who sought help in very personal and intimate parts of their lives. Angela was wearing a dark brown overcoat, buttoned to the neck, gloves and a hat to match with a brim, pulled down to shade her face. She was another wife who had found it impossible to respond to her husband's love making. He was remarkably tolerant, no doubt she would not have married him if he had been more masterful. Slowly by very small steps, her inhibitions were broken down; unlock the bathroom door, talk to Jim while you are in there; let him sit on the toilet seat while you are in the hedgehog position in the bath; let him soap your back; go to bed in a nightdress instead of pyjamas, step by step she learnt to accept the normal contacts of intimacy. Jim never gave up and never exceeded his brief. He knew it would be disastrous if he did and after about nine months his patience was rewarded and full intercourse took place. She was a religious woman and I am sure the change would not have happened if she had not been motivated by the belief, as I pointed out to her, that God would not have encouraged mankind to be fruitful and multiply if he had not intended a sexual relationship to be essential to marriage. What she had not expected was that the experience could be enjoyable!

'What on earth have you done to that couple?' asked the receptionist

'Why?'

'Well you'd hardly know they were the same people that came here first last year – she's got no hat or gloves, the dowdy coat has gone and she's wearing a pink V-necked blouse and a green skirt! They even hold hands in the waiting room!'

Women were not my only patients and many an embarrassed male, almost always on his own, walked hesitantly to the chair at the side of my desk.

'How can I help you?'

'Well, it's kind of awkward, know what I mean. . . '

'Most of the men I see either can't get it up or come too quick.'

Relief at these down-to-earth alternatives nearly always loosened their tongues.

'Yes, that's just it. I can't hold on. . .'

'Good!' He looked astonished.

'I'm delighted that it's premature ejaculation that's troubling you because we have a very good treatment for it. It's nothing to do with squeezing your penis or excercises with your partner, it's just some pills. . .'

I would give the man a private prescription for amitryptiline, as very few wanted their GPs to know anything about it (although they had to be told if other medication was prescribed) and very specific instructions on gradually increasing the dose, maintenance for a month and slow withdrawal of the drug, with a mid-cycle phone call to me to report progress. Failures were few and occasional relapses could be treated with more of the same. These men were usually young and fit but with a basic lack of confidence which was demonstrated just when they wanted to show themselves at their most virile.

Erectile failure was the curse of the older man, most commonly when his arteries were hardening from high blood pressure or diabetes and the blood supply to his penis was not as good as it should be. Sometimes there were psychogenic factors and the difficulty lay in distinguishing the two groups. It was possible, by injecting a drug into the shaft of the organ, to stimulate an erection if there were was no underlying organic disease. We had an excellent arrangement with the Department of Urology at the Western Infirmary whereby patients could attend at 5 p.m. for this 'test'. The resulting erection was substantial and lasted for over half an hour. We would advise the man to arrange for his wife to be available when he returned home, to make the best use of it while it lasted. In practice, many regained their lost confidence and one treatment was enough.

I usually had a good idea of whether the erectile failure was organic, due to vascular or neural damage or was 'functional' ie, psychogenic but I was not always right.

Robert was a good looking man in his forties. He and his fiancée came to see me together as he was quite unable to produce even a flicker of response from his penis however much they both desired it. He was the only son of a widowed mother and had lived at home all his life. She had been very possessive and had successfully thwarted all his attempts to have a girlfriend, let alone contemplate marriage. She had died the previous year and now he and his 28 year old partner did not want to waste any more time. They both wanted a successful sexual relationship and hoped to have a family but agreed that unless Robert's problem could be solved they should not embark on marriage.

Here was the classic psychogenic explanation and the injection trial should do the trick and restore his seriously eroded confidence. It failed completely, but the lack of response led the urologist to investigate further. Robert had been born with a vascular abnormality which prevented the penis from hardening up. Happily this was corrected by surgery and, although his performance was never as good as James Bond, it was entirely adequate and he and his Alison were joyfully joined in matrimony.

I had several patients whose idea of their own self worth was centred on their ability to complete the sexual act. They were prepared to wear the most uncomfortable contraptions, even to undergo painful operations in order to produce the necessary erection and achieve penetration. That era is now in the dark ages B.V. – Before Viagra. This drug must seem like a miracle to tens of thousands of men who despaired of ever having a full sexual relationship again.

Many of the couples and individuals who attended our special sessions were unhappy in their relationship or had intractable personality problems but I think nearly all of them benefited from talking out their difficulties in a non-judgemental atmosphere. Whether this is what is known as 'counselling' I cannot judge, but I prefer to avoid the term whenever possible. Sexual inhibitions in both sexes were widespread in the sixties and seventies and, while all child abuse is abhorrent, it is persistant molestation by someone close to the child which does the lasting damage.

Joan was brought reluctantly by her husband because of her 'frigidity'. She tolerated intercourse but was unable to respond.

'I feel as though I'm committing rape,' he confessed.

'Don't say that. You know I don't mind really,' she protested.

'Has it always been like this?' I asked

'Oh yes, and she would never let me touch her in that way until we were married – and it's not much better now,' he said.

'Have you any idea why you feel this way?' I asked her.

She looked down and lowered her voice 'I had a nasty experience when I was ten'

'What happened?'

'Must I tell you?'

'Yes, it will really be a great help. You'll feel a lot better once you've put it into words.'

'Well, it was about five o'clock and nearly dark and my mum asked me to go down the stair to borrow a cup of sugar from our neighbour who lived in the same close.' She paused.

'Yes. . .'

'Well, when I was coming back with the sugar, there was a man on the half landing and he stood in front of me so that I couldn't go past him,' she stopped again.

'Go on.'

'He had his flies undone and his thing stuck out – it was huge, I didn't realise what it was at first. He tried to make me touch it but I screamed and managed to run upstairs.'

'Did you know him?'

'Yes, but only slightly. He lived in the next close.'

'What happened then?'

'My mum said I was wicked to say such a thing about Mr Munro and I was making it up. She said I had no business to know anything about his thing and I was a dirty girl and should be ashamed of myself. She beat me with a chair leg.'

It did not take long to find out that she had been brought up to think of sex as dirty and nakedness as sinful. The flasher on the stair had only reinforced all her bad feelings about sexuality. It was no wonder she had difficulty responding to her husband but it was much easier for her to blame the single episode of abuse, even though it did not involve any physical trauma, than face the truth –

that her problem lay in her own mother's misguided attitudes.

I hope that this type of psycho-sexual problem is now a thing of the past, ideals of purity and virginity are no longer 'cool', but I fear those who have really been traumatised by those they trusted are damaged, sometimes beyond repair and in their turn may seek relief by exploiting the vulnerable themselves.

My youngest daughter was pulled in beside the dustbins by a man who exposed himself to her on her way home from school. Although she had a fright, what she remembers best was the ride round the neighbourhood in the police car to see if she could spot him. Z-cars was all the rage on the telly at the time. I told her the man was sick in his mind and could not really help it but he had to be caught to stop him frightening other children. She seemed happy with this explanation and certainly had no hang-ups afterwards. The person who was most upset and made the biggest fuss was my 'daily' woman, who worked in my house in the afternoons so that she was there when the children came home from school.

I had patients of both sexes who had had some appalling experiences but the lasting trauma was not only because of the physical hurts but because these had been inflicted by those who were supposed to love and care for them – stepfathers, uncles, brothers, grandfathers, and, most wounding of all, frequently with the connivance of their mothers. The most important message to get across to the victims was that it was not their fault. Guilt compounded their disgust, they must have 'led on' the man. Even women who had first been sexually abused when small children, blamed themselves.

Re-establishing a sense of their own self-worth was difficult and sometimes beyond my skills.

Nowadays our psychotherapists are properly trained and most large centres provide good facilities for those with sexual problems, but how I wish I had not retired B.V. (Before Viagra).

No Men Allowed

'Lubby, have ye got anything fur toothache?' I was sitting in the corner of a dimly lit room, chairs ranged against the wall with just enough space for a low coffee table in the middle. It opened out of a small lobby with a locked door onto the street. There were no windows. Beside me was a narrow passage about eight feet long, which ended in a door. Beyond this lay the 'medical room', about seven by four (feet) within which was an examination couch, a chair and two wall-mounted cupboards. There was just room for the doctor or nurse and the patient.

'I think I've got some oil of cloves and I can give you two paracetamol.'

'Okay.'

'Come with me and I'll give them to you.' The sixteen year old prostitute followed me down the passage.

'Put your fag out. There's no smoking down this end.'

Fire was a very real hazard. There was only one way out of the premises, through the locked front door. All the clients and most of the social workers smoked obsessively while they were in the Drop-in Centre. Many were high on drugs or alcohol and virtually all carried an offensive weapon of a sharpened kind down their boot or in their handbag. The only heating came from an old-fashioned three-bar electric fire balanced across the seat of a chair, as the flex would not otherwise reach the ceiling-high socket. This chair was placed diagonally so that the fire projected into the open end of the corridor and provided a constant hazard to anyone going down to the medical room. I had bought two fireproof blankets that were fixed outside the door of my cubby hole. I reckoned that if fire broke out and we were trapped the only way to prevent incineration was to fling a blanket over our heads and charge through. It was as well that no Health and Safety Inspector examined the premises or it would have been closed immediately.

The Drop-in Centre in Holme Street was the result of two initiatives, one by concerned social workers and the other by certain doctors and nurses employed by the Greater Glasgow Health Board. We were all involved with young drug users, many of whom used prostitution to fund their habit. Young women in these circum-stances find it almost impossible to attend clinics or their GPs, yet most had medical problems, sometimes very serious, which needed treatment. Many were already known to the social services because of their own or their children's needs. We were also concerned to encourage them to use condoms and to increase their knowledge of how HIV and AIDS were spread. By combining two small-scale pre-existing projects into the Centre at Holme Street, a viable and increasingly popular resource was established. It was staffed by two, subsequently three, social workers who supplied the coffee and the cheese sandwiches, supervised the running of it and kept an eye on the clients. The Health Board supplied a nurse three evenings a week and a doctor for two. All the staff were on a rota as it was a demanding shift, from 8 p.m. until midnight and one never knew what the evening would bring.

I had seen the premises briefly and organised the supply of anticipated medical drugs and appliances with suitable locks on the door and the cupboards. Ten days later we were in business and I found my way down the sleazy back streets round the Finnieston Bus Station, parked the car without difficulty against the kerb, locked it up and looked up and down the unlit street. The premises had previously been used as a 'sauna' and seeing the faded letters over the closed door I rapped vigorously. The door opened. There was a lady behind the reception counter bare except for gold caps to her nipples (I could not see below her waist) with psychedelic orange and green strobe lighting providing the only illumination. I don't know who was the more surprised. It took a moment or two to realise that I had indeed entered a 'sauna' in the street sense of the term. What she thought of this elderly rather shabby old woman, clutching a large holdall, she did not say verbally but her expression was a mixture of horror and amazement.

'I'm terribly sorry, come to the wrong door. I'm looking for the Drop-in Centre.'

'That's alright, hen, two doors along.' She had recovered almost immediately and was smiling. We both laughed and I was shown out.

I confess it took some internal adjustment to be addressed by my Christian name by a young lassie who could be my grand-daughter, without giving any indication that I found it unusual. We were all on familiar terms and age and status were irrelevant but I believed my white hair did have some effect on the volatile clientele. No fights or open aggression were manifest while 'old granny' was sitting in the corner.

Toothache was the least of the medical problems. Apart from the obvious requests for pregnancy tests, cervical smears, check-ups for venereal diseases and supplies of the pill or the contra-ceptive injection, there were more unusual demands. One woman had had her throat superficially cut and the eighteen beautifully fine stitches inserted at the Royal had already been in too long as she had never managed to return to Casualty. Fortunately they were not yet infected and were easily removed. Another seventeen year old had fallen backwards onto an open fire when she had a fit after injecting a cocktail of 'jellies' and 'tems'. She had several suppurating burns on her back that should have been regularly dressed but her partner, or rather her pimp, had abandoned her and she could not manage to deal with them herself.

Many of our clients were already HIV-positive and some had full-blown AIDS. In 1989 there was little effective treatment for the virus but the associated infections could usually be dealt with. On several occasions I had to telephone the AIDS unit at Ruchill Hospital and ask for the admission of a really sick patient.

There were boxes of condoms in the lobby of many varieties. It had become apparent to me in the mid eighties that one of the few practical ways of decreasing the spread of the HIV virus was to increase the use of condoms. It became our policy to supply boxes, usually containing a gross, to all outlets which were in contact with at-risk groups. Drug centres and subsequently needle exchange centres regularly collected them from Claremont Terrace or members of the Domiciliary team who worked in the area handed them in. We did not demand that records should be kept of whom they were given to, or how many at a time.

The Drop-in Centre was the ideal place in which to locate a depot of these free supplies but I had a lot to learn about our clients needs before we found the right assortment. 'Blow jobs', the woman 'sucking off' the man's penis, were very popular with the prostitutes and their clients as the risk of catching the AIDS virus were much less than with full genital penetration. The price was correspondingly less. Nearly all condoms are lubricated with a spermicide, nonoxynol-9, but this has a far from alluring taste. On the other hand I did not think the Greater Glasgow Health Board should be providing strawberry or chocolate flavoured licks to make the work of these service providers more palatable. We found that non-lubricated condoms, without the commercial packaging or the titillating names, could be bought in large quantities very cheaply as they are provided for patients with urinary tract problems.

Peggy consulted me about an itchy rash on her right hand. It stretched from the base of her index finger across the palm and extended onto the fleshy base of her thumb. Nonoxynol-9 not only tastes nasty it can also cause an allergic rash. Peggy offered 'hand jobs' as part of her stock in trade. This was the first case of 'prostitute's palm' that I saw but by no means the last. I have always regretted that I did not have a camera. It would have made a nice little item for the Minerva miscellany on the back page of the *British Medical Journal*. In an earlier era it might even have earned a footnote as 'Wilson's dermatitis' in a Handbook of Dermatology!

I had observed in my time at the V.D. clinic in Sheffield that rumours about the relative sizes of the penis in different races were basically true. In the late eighties all the condoms were a standard size and this was too small for some Afro-Caribbeans and too big for some Asians (although size has nothing to do with performance). Nowadays there is a range of different condoms (up to ten varieties from one manufacturer alone), to suit the individual but I don't expect most of the professional ladies have time to be very selective in the back of a car in the dark.

Most of the women who came to the centre were very aware of the risks of HIV although some, especially the young drug addicts, were prepared to agree to unprotected genital intercourse, at a price. Many said they insisted on their clients using 'rubbers' but this did not extend to their regular boyfriends.

'But, Sandra, do you **always** use a condom?'

'Yes, of course. I lose a bit of money but it's safer that way.'

'So you don't have sex with **anyone** unless you are protected?'

'That's right. Except for Pete, know what I mean?'

'What do you mean, 'except for Pete'?'

'Well, he's ma boyfriend and that's different.'

'What do you mean 'different'? He might be positive or you might be and then you'd infect each other.'

'No, no, you don't understand. We trust each other and if I asked him to use a rubber he would think I thought he'd been with someone else. He knows I go with punters but always with a condom. He trusts me and I trust him and that's it.'

However misplaced that trust, there was no persuading her – in fact I did not even try. We all have to work within our own codes of behaviour.

One Wednesday evening not long after the Drop-in had opened I noticed a woman in her early twenties. She inhaled deeply from her cigarette and as she raised her head to exhale the smoke our eyes met. She smiled.

'It's you, Dr Wilson.'

'Certainly is, and I know you. You're a McNemeny. I'd know those blue eyes anywhere.'

'I'm Anna.'

'Does your mum still live in Langholm Street?'

'Yeh, I remember when you used to come and visit before she was sterilised.'

I remembered her mum very well. Anna was one of twelve children, one of the older girls, but they all had the same extraordinarily bright blue, rather flat, eyes. Three or four years before I had literally bumped into a boy of about nine as I came, laden, through the doors of a supermarket. It was not his fault and as I was apologising I said, 'You must be a McNemeny.' He stared.

'How do you know?'

'It's those wonderful blue eyes. Tell your mum Dr Wilson was asking after her.'

Now, here was another of her children, obviously in trouble and far from well. I remembered seeing the mantelpiece edged with little piles of coins, dinner money for at least six of her family, carefully put on one side when she returned from the post office with her children's allowances. She was a loving, caring, capable mother, overwhelmed by sheer numbers. Even with the exchange of their old three apartment flat for a four bedroomed maisonette, they were still grossly overcrowded.

Anna was addicted to heroin and anything else she could acquire and fed her habit by selling herself while her boyfriend watched her back. Sometimes the only drugs they could get were in tablet form. These were ground up between two spoons, stirred with water and injected intravenously. Naturally the lining of the abused veins would react and become inflamed. This usually resulted in their becoming solid with infected blood clots, 'thrombosed up' as the jargon had it. Anna only had one available vein in her body – in her neck. She told me she had to lie on the sofa with her head hanging down over the edge 'to bring the vein up' and her partner would then give her the injection. She had been on two 'rehab' (rehabilitation) courses which both succeeded for a short time but then the craving and the continued drug usage by her 'pals' overcame her common sense and she started again, only by now she was HIV-positive.

One girl had not been long discharged after an attack of pneumocystis carinii pneumonia. It was a foul night, bitterly cold and stormy. When the door was unlocked in response to her frantic knocking, she stumbled in, wet, bedraggled and painfully thin, shivering and wracked by a persistent cough.

'Dinnae let him get me.'

'It's okay, no men are allowed in here. You know we only unlock the door to women who identify themselves.'

'He sez Ah've gottae work, but Ah cannae staun up.'

'You're safe here. You're not well. How long have you had that cough?'

'Ah got took intae the hospital wi' pneumonia but they let me oot last week. Ah wiznae right but he wanted me oot and Ah said Ah wouldnae stay.'

'So now you've got worse. Shall I ask the ward to take you back?'

'Oh, aye, Ah think Ah'll dee if Ah have tae gang oot tae the street again the night.'

'Sister, I've got Donna Campbell here at the Drop-in. She's pretty sick.'

'That's fine, Doctor, we know her well. I'm not surprised she's relapsed. She discharged herself last week – no doubt under pressure from that awful man she stays with.'

'Will it be alright if I bring her along about half past twelve? I must be here until midnight, but that's not long now?'

'No, that's fine. Just come straight to the ward and knock on the door. I'll be expecting you.'

Soon after midnight I shepherded Donna into my car and set off for Ruchill.

'Would ye mind stopping aff at an all-night garage?' she asked.

'Whatever for?'

'Well, you see Ah've gottae get ma fags and Ah'm awfy thirsty and Ah could do wi' a can o' Irn-Bru.'

'That's okay. But I don't know where to find an all-night garage.'

'Na, but Ah dae. There's one on St George's Road, we'll be passing that.'

So I duly pulled in and Donna got her essential supplies before we arrived at the hutted ward. A knock on the door, a friendly face and she slipped inside, out of the cold and wet and away from the threatening presence of her 'protector', at least for a few days.

Maggie was another regular customer. I believe she was only twenty-eight but she looked fifty. She had a child, Gemma, who was three. The child stayed with her grandmother but Maggie lived there too when she was not either in Corntonvale (the women's prison) or in hospital for the recurrent AIDS-related problems that afflicted her. Maggie's whole life was concentrated on this little girl. She would pass round photographs of her dressed in grotesque parodies of adult finery, frocks covered in sequins or made of gold lame – where she got them from it was impossible to guess. Every week she would buy some gold adornment, ear rings, bangles, necklaces, pendants so that if the child had worn them all simultaneously she would hardly have been able to move for the weight. As the date of Gemma's birthday drew nearer, Maggie told us of the huge party she was giving for her – hiring a hall and a band. She was not sure what her birthday present was going to be because she already had a TV and video in her bedroom.

Maggie knew she had a fatal illness and it was heart-rending to see her showering this small girl with, literally, all her money could buy. She worked the streets when she was so ill she could hardly walk regardless of the bitter winds and constant rain. It was far too late to tell her that what her daughter really needed was her mother's presence in her life and that the inappropriate gifts and clothing would only alienate her from the other children in the neighbourhood.

One night there was a frenzied knocking on the door and when it was opened Maggie collapsed against the door-jamb. She was wet to the skin and both her legs were enormously swollen, especially the left. When she had taken off her shoes to relieve the pain she could not get them on again. She was shivering with fever and once we had helped her into the little medical room and given her a hot mug of coffee, I was able to find out what the immediate problem was. All the superficial veins in her legs were thrombosed and this in itself results in severe oedema (swelling due to fluid retained in the tissues) but in her desperation to find a vein she had tried to inject the one in her groin. She had misplaced the needle and a jet of arterial blood had been forced into the muscles of her thigh. She had attended Casualty with this several nights before. The bleeding had stopped spontaneously (arteries have very elastic walls) but there was a huge bruise resulting from the underlying clot of extravasated blood, trapped below her groin. She was given pain killers and told to return the next day. This she failed to do and the clot became infected, no doubt from the dirty needle which had caused the original injury. Now she had a large suppurating abscess at the site. Walking was almost, but not totally impossible, and Maggie was another patient who ended up for the umpteenth time in the compassionate care of the staff at Ruchill.

As I drove her to the hospital she sobbed bitterly. Gemma's long planned and extremely expensive party was the next day and her mother knew there was no way she could be there.

Not long after this episode I was invited to go to Sierra Leone to work woth Marie Stopes International, the contraceptive aid agency that was establishing polyclinics in tha part of Africa. I immediately accepted as I felt that I had accomplished as much as I could in Glasgow. Differences of opinion with Greater Glasgow Helath Board had been temporariily patched up but I believed that new blood and new ideas were needed for the next decade before the challenges of the new millennium. I had had the good fortune to have been born in 1926 and had experienced medical life before a free health service. The NHS was established while I was a medical student in 1948 and the subsequent decades saw profound developments that brought medicine out of the dark ages into modern technology in diagnosis and treatment. These were exciting times fo r medical practitioners and my generataion were still able to practise the arts of human communication and compassion which now seem in danger. We were also largely free from committees and constraints imposed by political correctness and concerns about litigation. In common with many of my fellow paractitioners, I believe we had 'the best of times'.

ౚఀౚఀౚఀ

Index

Other Books
from Argyll Publishing

The Wind in her Hands
Margaret Gillies Brown
ISBN:1 902831 41 1 pbk £7.99

'an intriguing picture of life early last century' **Caledonia**

'it never flags – the story of a strong woman' **Moray Firth Radio**

'inspirational' **Press & Journal**

Tobermory Days
– stories from an island
Lorn Macintyre
ISBN 1 902831 56 X £7.99 paperback

'vivid and graceful. . . an excellent short story collection'
The Herald

'vibrant and vivid' **Sunday Herald**

'beautifully realised. . . compelling'
West Highland Free Press

Available in bookshops or direct from Argyll Publishing,
Glendaruel, Argyll PA22 3AE Scotland
For credit card, full stock list and other enquiries
tel 01369 820229   argyll.publishing@virgin.net
or visit our website www.skoobe.biz